THE FUTURE OF BURMA

Crisis and Choice in Myanmar

January 1990 —

D1824597

The Asia Society is a nonprofit, nonpartisan public education organization dedicated to increasing U.S. understanding of Asia and its growing importance to the United States and to world relations. Founded in 1956, the Society covers all of Asia—30 countries from Japan to Iran and from Soviet Central Asia to the South Pacific Islands. Through its programs in contemporary affairs, the fine and performing arts, and elementary and secondary education, the Society reaches audiences across the United States and works closely with colleagues in Asia.

The Education and Contemporary Affairs Division of The Asia Society seeks to

- Alert Americans to the key Asian issues of the 1990s

- Illuminate the policy choices facing decision makers in the public and private sectors

- Strengthen the dialogue between Americans and Asians on the issues and their policy implications

The division identifies issues in consultation with a group of advisers and addresses these issues through studies and publications, national and international conferences, public programs around the United States, and corporate and media activities. The division receives funding from the Ford Foundation, the Henry Luce Foundation, the Andrew W. Mellon Foundation, Mr. and Mrs. George O'Neill, the Rockefeller Brothers Fund, and Mr. David Rockefeller.

THE FUTURE OF BURMA

Crisis and Choice in Myanmar

by David I. Steinberg

UNIVERSITY PRESS OF AMERICA

LANHAM • NEW YORK • LONDON

Copyright © 1990 by
University Press of America®, Inc.
4720 Boston Way
Lanham, Maryland 20706

3 Henrietta Street
London WC2E 8LU England

Co-published by arrangement with
The Asia Society,
725 Park Avenue, New York, New York 10021

Library of Congress Cataloging-in-Publication Data

Steinberg, David I.
The future of Burma.

(Asian agenda report ; 14)
Includes bibliographical references.
1. Burma—History—1948–   . I. Title.
II. Series.
DS530.4.S74   1990   959.105   90–11974

ISBN 0–8191–7777–6 (alk. paper)
ISBN 0–8191–7778–4 (pbk. : alk. paper)

 The paper used in this publication meets the minimum requirements of
American National Standard for Information Sciences—Permanence
of Paper for Printed Library Materials, ANSI Z39.48–1984.

Contents

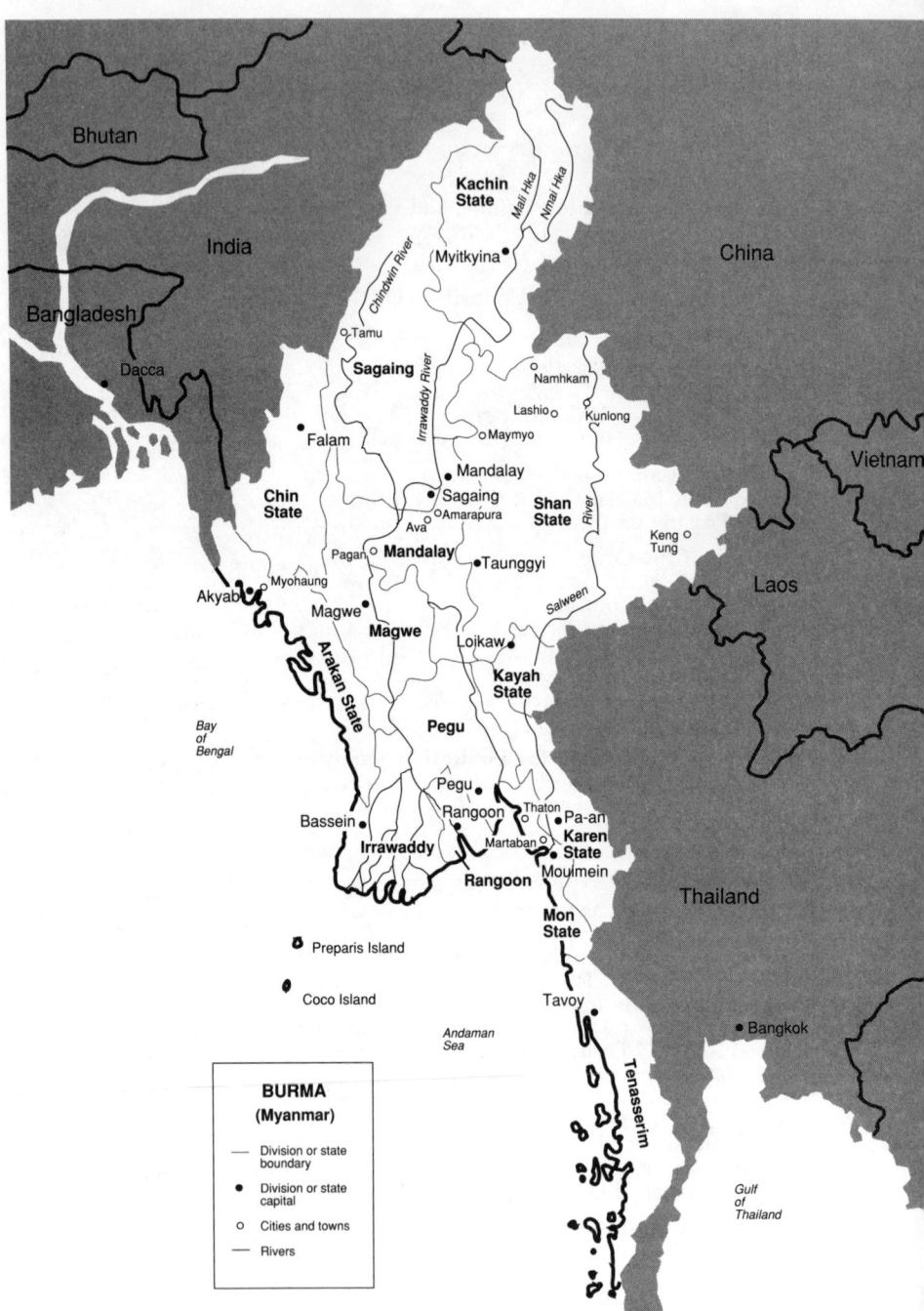

Bhutan

India

Bangladesh

Dacca

China

Kachin
State

Myitkyina

Mali Hka
Nmai Hka

Chindwin River

Tamu

Sagaing

Irrawaddy River

Namhkam

Lashio
Maymyo
Kunlong

Falam

Chin
State

Mandalay

Sagaing
Amarapura
Ava

Shan
State

Salween River

Keng
Tung

Vietnam

Laos

Pagan
Myohaung

Mandalay

Taunggyi

Akyab

Magwe

Magwe

Loikaw

Kayah
State

Salween

Bay
of
Bengal

Arakan State

Pegu

Pegu

Bassein

Irrawaddy

Rangoon
Martaban

Thaton
Pa-an
Karen
State

Moulmein

Rangoon

Mon
State

Preparis Island

Coco Island

Tavoy

Andaman
Sea

Bangkok

Thailand

Tenasserim

Gulf
of
Thailand

BURMA
(Myanmar)

— Division or state
  boundary

● Division or state
  capital

○ Cities and towns

— Rivers

vi

Foreword

The question of whether Asia's Leninist societies will follow Eastern Europe's dramatic experiments in parliamentary democracy, or at least achieve a greater political openness, is surely unanswerable at this time. But it is a question that will just as surely be asked many times over in the period immediately ahead, as these societies, or more properly their authoritarian leaderships, see the communist system virtually breaking up before their very eyes and find themselves forced to confront serious challenges both internally and externally to their legitimacy.

One such test case is Burma, little known to the Western world but deserving of far greater attention. As this report goes to press, the people of Burma, recently renamed Myanmar, are preparing for elections for a 492-seat legislature that is supposed to write a new constitution. The scheduling of these elections for May 1990 was the result of a vigorous prodemocracy movement in Rangoon in the summer of 1988. Yet there are ominous signs today that the process of liberalizing the Burmese polity will continue long after the elections have been held, suggesting that as with the People's Republic of China, North Korea, and Vietnam, the road to basic political reform in Burma will be rocky indeed. The Asia Society is grateful to David I. Steinberg for his skillful handling of the historical and cultural factors underlying today's events in Burma as well as for his analysis of the events themselves in the timely report that follows.

The Future of Burma: Crisis and Choice in Myanmar is the latest in a series produced by The Asia Society's Education and Contemporary Affairs Division. The division seeks to alert Americans to critical issues in Asian affairs and in U.S.-Asian relations, to illuminate the choices that public and private policymakers face, and to strengthen transpacific dialogue on the issues. Through studies, national and international conferences, regional public programs in the United States, and corporate and media activities, the division involves U.S. and Asian specialists and opinion leaders in a far-reaching education process.

I wish to thank Deborah F. Washburn, senior editor in The Asia Society's recently reorganized Education and Contemporary Affairs Division, for her role in shepherding the project to completion. Her predecessor, Sarah H. Beckjord, and Terrence R. George, former assistant director of the Contemporary Affairs Department, worked closely with the author from the beginning to ensure an excellent product, with the able assistance of Andrea Sokerka, who has provided essential continuity and production expertise.

K. A. Namkung
Executive Director
Education and Contemporary Affairs Division
The Asia Society
January 1990

Acknowledgments

This work is dedicated to the peoples of Burma.

The author wishes to thank Robert Taylor of the School of Oriental and African Studies, University of London, Josef Silverstein of Rutgers University, and Bertil Lintner of the *Far Eastern Economic Review* for their very helpful comments on various drafts. All three have been stalwart writers on contemporary Burma, and their works are listed in the Suggested Reading section.

The nature of this volume precludes footnoting, and thus the author is not able to acknowledge those many individuals who have unknowingly influenced his work, nor can he thank those in Burma with whom he met over the past 30 years and on several recent trips and who inadvertently contributed to its content.

In spite of these various supports, the conclusions presented herein are those of the author alone and do not reflect the views of The Asia Society or any other institution or individual.

D. Steinberg
Bethesda, Maryland
January 1990

Notes on Names, Terms, Abbreviations, and Exchange Rates

Since independence in 1948, Burma's official name has changed three times. In 1948 it was the Union of Burma. After the 1962 coup it was renamed the Socialist Republic of the Union of Burma. Following the coup of 1988, the name reverted to its earlier form. In 1989, however, the military administration, to avoid ethnic labels, once again changed the name, this time to the Union of Myanmar (sometimes spelled without the "r," viz., Myanma). Myanmar has been the Burmese name of Burma since independence. Other names have been changed to conform to Burmese spelling: "Yangon" has replaced Rangoon, and "Rakhine" replaced Arakan. In this volume, Myanmar remains Burma for the convenience of foreign readers, and Rangoon and Arakan likewise retain their Western spellings.

The following name changes (in addition to those above) were announced by Myanmar Notification 5/89 of June 18, 1989:

	Old Name	New Name
Peoples	Karen	Kayin
	Burman	Bamar
	Arakanese	Rakhine (previously announced)
States/Divisions/	Pa-an	Hpa-an
Capitals	Moulmein	Mawlamyine
	Akyab	Sittwe (previously announced)
	Tennasserim	Tanintharyin
	Tavoy	Dawei
	Irrawaddy	Ayeyarwady (also a river)
	Bassein	Pathein
Rivers	Salween	Thanlwin
	Sittang	Sittoung
	Chindwin	Chindwinn

A wide variety of street name changes were also announced for Rangoon.

There are no surnames in Burma, and all individuals have their own names, which they maintain even after marriage. Names are normally prefaced with a title derived from family relations, the most common of which are "U" (uncle) for men and "Daw" (aunt) for women, indicating respect for mature males and females. Other titles, such as "elder brother," "younger brother," or "younger sister," are used as appropriate to indicate relationship, friendship, status, and age. In this essay all such titles have been eliminated except for (U) Nu and (U) Thant when first introduced, as these titles are sometimes inappropriately considered part of the name. Some names are quite common, such as Maung Maung or Tin Oo; three persons named Tin Oo are mentioned in this volume.

The term "Burman" is now commonly used in an ethnolinguistic sense to denote a person who speaks Burmese as a native language and adheres to the cultural norms of that majority group. A "Burmese," however, is any citizen of Burma, regardless of ethnicity.

The official exchange rate of the Burmese kyat (K) to the U.S. dollar has changed from about K4.70=US$1.00 in the 1950s to K6.00–K6.50=US$1.00 in the 1980s. In the latter period, the exchange rate has varied in accordance with the value of a basket of currencies used by the International Monetary Fund. The unofficial black-market exchange rate in 1988–89 was about K40–K45=US$1.00, although it varied daily and by location. By the summer of 1989, the black-market rate was about K50=US$1.00, and in the autumn of that year it was about K65=US$1.00.

Abbreviations and Special Terms

AFPFL	Anti-Fascist People's Freedom League
BCP	Burma Communist Party
BSPP	Burma Socialist Programme Party
GNP	Gross National Product
NUP	National Unity Party
SLORC	State Law and Order Restoration Council
Bogyoke	General, used of Aung San and Ne Win
lon htein	riot police
Pyithu Hluttaw	People's Assembly
sangha	Buddhist monkhood
sawbwa	Shan or Kayah ruler (akin to maharajah)
tatmadaw	Armed Forces of Burma

Key Figures

Alaungpaya	King (ruled 1752–1760).
Anawrahta	King (ruled 1044–1077).
Aung Gyi	(b. 1918) Brigadier. Anticolonial student leader; officer, 4th Burma Rifles; leader under Ne Win of caretaker government, 1958–1960; heir apparent to Ne Win, 1962–1963, later jailed and released; founded Union Nationals Democratic Party in 1988.
Aung San	(1916–1947) General. Father of independent Burma. Anticolonial student leader, later trained by Japanese; commander of army in WWII; negotiated Burmese independence from Britain; assassinated in 1947 before independence.
Aung San Suu Kyi	(b. 1945) Only daughter of Aung San. Scholarly expatriate married to an Englishman; returned to Burma to attend to her failing mother and became a general secretary of the National League for Democracy; until placed under house arrest on July 20, 1989, was the military's most vocal critic.
Aye Ko	General, formerly 4th Burma Rifles. Joint secretary, BSPP, until resignation in 1988.
Ba Swe	(1915–1978) Socialist leader. Student leader in anticolonial struggle; leader of Burma Socialist Party and AFPFL; prime minister, 1956–1957; also deputy prime minister and other portfolios. Split with Nu in 1958 and with Kyaw Nyein founded "Stable AFPFL."
Bo Mya	Karen leader of Karen National Defense Organization. Now chair, Democratic Alliance for Burma, in rebellion along Thai border.
Brang Sang	Kachin opposition leader. Now vice chair, Democratic Alliance for Burma.

Chit Hlaing	General. Former foreign minister under military; organizer of progovernment National Unity Party.
Khun Sa	Sino-Shan leader (real name Chang Chi-fu) of an antigovernment Shan rebellion and of the illegal opium trade.
Kyanzittha	King (ruled 1084–1112).
Kyaw Nyein	(1915–1987) Anti-British student activist and founding member of the Burma Socialist Party. Split with Nu in 1958 and joined with Ba Swe to form "Stable AFPFL."
Khin Nyunt	Brigadier general. Secretary of SLORC since coup of September 18, 1988; chief of the Directorate of Defense Services Intelligence; regarded as a power behind SLORC and a potential leader.
Maung Maung	(b. 1925) Civilian jurist. Editor, *Guardian* magazine, author of various books on the Burmese constitution, and biographer of Ne Win; author of much of the military's legislation. President and chair, BSPP, August–September 1988.
Ne Win	(b. 1911) A leader of anti-British struggle. Member with Aung San of "30 Comrades" trained by Japanese in 1941; commander, 4th Burma Rifles; deputy commander, Burma army, 1948, commander beginning 1949; several times defense minister; prime minister, 1958–1960; leader of 1962 coup. Since 1962 chief figure in Burma as, variously, chair, Revolutionary Council, 1962–1974; president, 1974–1981; founder and chair, BSPP, 1962–1988.

Nu	(b. 1907) Civilian leader. Anticolonial student leader; after assassination of Aung San became Burma's first prime minister, 1948–1956, 1957–1962; president, AFPFL; leader, "Clean AFPFL," 1958, Union Party, 1960–1962. Led rebellion against Ne Win from Thailand, was granted amnesty, and returned to Burma, where he worked on Buddhist texts and, in 1988, became patron of League for Democracy and Peace.
San Yu	(b. 1918) General, formerly 4th Burma Rifles. Secretary, Revolutionary Council; president, 1981–1988; vice chair, BSPP. Until 1988, heir to Ne Win.
Saw Maung	(b. 1928) General. Commander: Northern Command, 1978, Southwestern Command, 1979; vice chief-of-staff, Burma army, 1983; deputy defense minister, 1984; chief-of-staff, Defense Services, 1985. Titular coup leader and chair, SLORC, since coup of September 18, 1988.
Sein Lwin	General. Enlisted 4th Burma Rifles. Responsible for firing on students, 1962, 1974, and March 1988. Became chair, BSPP, and president, July 1988; forced to resign, August 1988.
Shu Maung	Original name of Ne Win.
Thant	(1909–1974) Statesman. Secretary to Nu; ambassador to U.N., 1957; secretary-general, U.N., 1961–1971.

Tin Oo	(b. 1923) General, chief-of-staff. In 1976, appeared to be successor to Ne Win. Jailed in 1976 for knowledge of a planned coup against Ne Win. Now chair, National League for Democracy, but under house arrest since July 20, 1989, and jailed again in December 1989. (Not to be confused with Brigadier General Tin Oo of SLORC, nor with General Tin Oo, former intelligence chief, dismissed in 1983 and subsequently jailed; released in October 1989.)
Tin Pe	Brigadier, 4th Burma Rifles. Architect of intense nationalization program of 1963, and at that time considered Ne Win's heir. Dismissed before first BSPP congress in 1971.

State Law and Order Restoration Council (SLORC)
September 1988

General Saw Maung	Chairman, SLORC; armed forces commander-in-chief; minister of defense; minister of foreign affairs; b. 1928.
Brig. General Myint Aung	Southwestern regional commander; b. 1932.
Lt. General Tha Shwe	Commander-in-chief, army; b. 1933.
Brig. General Myo Nyunt	Rangoon Command commander; b. 1930.
Brig. General Maung Thint	Northeastern regional commander; b. 1932.
Brig. General Khin Nyunt	Secretary, SLORC; b. 1939.
Brig. General Mya Thin	Western regional commander; b. 1931.
Brig. General Aye Thaung	Central regional commander; b. 1930.
Brig. General Aung Ye Kyaw	Armed forces adjutant general; minister of construction; minister of cooperatives; b. 1930.
Maj. General Sein Aung	Minister of industries I and II; chief, Bureau of Special Operations; b. 1933.
Maj. General Chit Swe	Chief, Bureau of Special Operations II; minister of livestock, breeding, and fisheries; minister of agriculture and forests; b. 1932.

Maj. General Tin Tun	Air Force commander-in-chief; minister of transport and communications; minister of social welfare and labor; b. 1930.
Maj. General Phone Myint	Minister for home and religious affairs; minister for information and culture; quartermaster general; b. 1931.
Rear Adm. Maung Maung Khin	Navy chief-of-staff; minister of mines; minister of energy; b. 1929.
Brig. General Tin Oo	Army chief-of-staff; secretary II, SLORC; b. 1933.
Brig. General Tun Kyi	Northeastern regional commander; b. 1938.
Brig. General Kyaw Ba	Northern regional commander; b. 1932.
Brig. General Maung Aye	Eastern regional commander; b. 1937.
Brig. General Nyan Lin	Southeastern regional commander; b. 1938.
Colonel David O. Abel	Minister of trade; minister of planning and finance.
Dr. Pe Thein	Minister of health and education.

Executive Summary

The military coup of September 18, 1988, the third in Burma's modern history, was different from most coups. The action in Burma was designed not to overthrow a failing government but to shore up a regime overwhelmed by popular protests. The violence associated with the coup and its aftermath was devastating to Burma's people, who had already suffered increasingly intolerable political and economic conditions. In 1988 alone, between 4,000 and 5,000 people were killed in the demonstrations and repressions.

Throughout Burma's postcolonial history, General Ne Win has played a critical role. He has variously functioned as commander of the armed forces, deputy prime minister, prime minister, and minister of defense, as well as chairman of the Revolutionary Council, president, and chairman of the state's only legal political party. For better or worse, no other figure in modern Burma can match his influence. After Ne Win retired as president in 1981, he retained a critical role as chairman of the Burma Socialist Programme Party, which he founded in 1962. Although he finally retired from that post on July 23, 1988, and his only current official title is "Patron of the War Veterans Organization," he retains power over many critical government decisions, functioning as a sort of Burmese Cardinal Richelieu. Ne Win's whim has been law in Burma, with the result that his subordinates have attempted to shield him from reality in order to show progress and avoid his wrath.

There is considerable continuity between Burma's imperial past and its more recent civilian and military periods. This heritage includes a strong centrist tendency that was initially the symbolic legacy of the monarchy and was later reinforced by the colonial government's effective administration within newly defined state boundaries. Even during Burma's civilian periods (1948–58 and 1960–62), when peripheral areas enjoyed modest local autonomy, the real power was located at the center, in Burman hands.

This centralization has been characteristic of Burma's economy as well. Upon independence, it was assumed that Burma would be socialist, and until recently the concept was not questioned; rather, what was at stake was the degree and effectiveness of nationalization.

Power has always been intensely personal in Burma; loyalty within the government is to the person, not the institution. Burma never developed an indigenous, institutionalized civil service based on merit. Because loyalty is personal, political parties have generally been devoted to their leaders rather than to programs as such; therefore, factionalism has also been characteristic of the Burmese political process. Thus politics in Burma has assumed primacy over other realms, vitiating economic and other reforms.

In 1988 Burma was in the midst of a revolution that was threatening the power of the elites: the military and the monied civilians. This revolution was the culmination of years of economic and political malaise and frustration. The economic degradation to which Burma had sunk was evident in December 1987, when Burma was declared one of the least-developed nations by the United Nations. Even Ne Win recognized the need for change. By September 1987 he had initiated two contradictory moves. First he freed the grain trade, most importantly rice, from government control in the most sweeping economic liberalization since 1962. Then, a few days later, he demonetized 70 percent of the country's currency, turning the economy into a shambles and encouraging inflation, hoarding, smuggling, and the opium trade.

Meanwhile, Burma's macroeconomic picture was poor: external debt had risen to about US$5 billion, partly from indiscreet borrowing and partly from loans coming due and the revaluation of the Japanese yen and the deutsche mark; internal debt was high due to poorly performing state economic enterprises; export values were down; and imports had fallen, thus depriving Burmese industry of raw materials and spare parts. At this point the Japanese quietly indicated to the Burmese that economic reforms were necessary.

At the same time, political frustration with the single-party system that affected the life of virtually every citizen was widespread. Both the party and society had become stratified: party loyalty was more important than competence; the children of the military elite received special privileges which set them apart from other students and youth, whose economic problems were acute.

Tensions rose in March 1988, when an apolitical student incident was put down with extreme brutality by the security police. The riots spread to downtown Rangoon, and 41 people suffocated to death in a police van. General Sein Lwin was held responsible by the students.

Demonstrations, resulting in many deaths, broke out again in mid-June, compounded by economic problems: inflation and unemployment. Rice prices were rising, because peasants held rice rather than cash. The government had to act.

Ne Win called for a party congress, which was held on July 23. He and four colleagues resigned their positions, a major economic liberalization program was announced, and Sein Lwin, much to the anger of the students, was chosen as both president and party chairman. Violent demonstrations ensued and spread throughout the country. On August 12, Sein Lwin was forced to resign. The following week Dr. Maung Maung, a civilian and close associate of Ne Win, was chosen for both positions.

But the political ferment could not be stopped. Massive demonstrations continued around the nation. The government had lost control of the administration. Finally, at a critical point when military morale seemed on the verge of collapse, a coup was staged to support the regime.

Since the September 18 coup, the military has been ruling by martial law, under the name of the State Law and Order Restoration Council (SLORC). The SLORC brutally suppressed all dissent, killing hundreds, perhaps thousands, in the effort, and forcing some ten thousand students to flee to the borders, where several thousand still remain. Arrests have continued sporadically.

The military has scheduled an election for May 1990. An election law was promulgated, and by March 1, 1989, 233 political parties had registered, of which 207 remain in December 1989. Economic liberalization has proceeded in Burma under a new foreign investment law, and the state has made major short-term trading deals with foreign firms to provide needed foreign exchange. Burma has also regularized the border smuggling trade with China, and it plans to do the same with Thailand. The single-party political system has been dismantled, a new government-sponsored (but not supported) party, the National Unity Party (NUP), has been formed, and the term "socialist" as a slogan has been discarded.

Although many in the opposition question whether free elections can or will take place under the military, some key political figures have emerged. These include Aung San Suu Kyi and General Tin Oo, retired, in one party (the former is now under house arrest for one year; the latter was sentenced in December 1989 to three years in jail), U Nu (now under house arrest) in another, and Brigadier Aung Gyi, retired, in a third. The amalgamation of the parties has begun, with many of the smaller parties that represent local or ethnic interests bringing their constituencies into larger groups.

The SLORC has searched for legitimacy inside and outside Burma. It has emphasized the humaneness of the military by providing welfare shops that supply low-priced rice and by giving substantial pay raises to the lower echelons of the civil service. Foreign newspaper reporters have been allowed into the country on occa-

3

sion although the Burmese press remains controlled and public criticism severely circumscribed.

The SLORC has also sought diplomatic contacts and the resumption of foreign assistance, which was halted on human rights grounds by most nations and multilateral organizations. In February 1989, Japan resumed its support for preexisting projects. Thailand has negotiated concessions for teak and fishing rights that raise significant environmental questions but bring quick foreign exchange into Burma. To ensure rice supplies for both internal use and exports, the government has reverted to a system that forces farmers to sell paddy to the state at below-market prices but at significantly lower volumes than before 1987.

The underlying crisis in the Burmese political economy has complex causes. These include the stratification of the social system, with the military controlling other avenues of mobility while retaining centralized power. Urbanization has increased the problem of unemployment, which is widespread. The government has unobtrusively allowed citizens to leave the country in order to defuse urban unrest, and has thereby drained the state of talent.

The Burmese state has historically been *dirigiste*—that is, it has controlled all economic and social matters—and so it remains. At significant points in the past it has attempted economic liberalization, but always with less effect than planned because of political factors. This present crisis offers more hope for economic reform and raises the possibility of a multiparty system, which would be a significant and major change.

The Burmese have long held ambivalent views on foreign involvement and have regarded the external world with suspicion mixed with cultural pride. Yet advances in technology and communications mean that Burma can no longer be isolated from the world outside.

Burma's choices for the future fall into two categories: those concerning internal center-periphery relations and those concerning Burma's relations with the outside world.

Burma must come to grips with the distribution of power. Whatever government is formed must develop a new constitution reflecting that decision. Indications point to the military holding control of the state apparatus during this process. In any case, its influence will be critical.

The most important issues for Burma are the role of the state and the role of ethnicity. The former finds expression in the debate over a unitary versus a federal system of government in a multiparty state. Ethnic tensions have been expressed in extreme form by rebellions of minorities in peripheral areas of the country. Burma must cope with these rebellions in order to deal with the internal allocation of budgetary resources and with the flourishing narcotics trade. But neither the narcotics problem nor the larger issue of the role of minorities will be solved by the elimination of the rebellions alone. The government will have to confront the question of minority participation in the economy and encourage legal economic activities in the peripheral regions, which contain much of the state's natural resources. The ethnic situation is complicated by the existence of foreign minorities—Chinese and Indians—who in the past have controlled much of Burma's economy. Civilian-military relations and the question of how to move from a military regime to a civilian government are also exceedingly difficult for Burma, as for a number of other states.

Internationally, Burma has been the neutralist country *par excellence*, but the military has interpreted neutrality as isolationism. The tensions will be severe as Burma attempts to preserve its traditions and simultaneously modernize its economy, which requires increased foreign trade and investment, as well as foreign aid and advanced technology that depends upon outside technical assistance and training abroad.

Burma's most important economic relations have been with Japan, which until recently supplied about half of all foreign aid. China now dominates the illegal and legalized border trade, although Thailand has made a strong bid to increase its influence through trading and close relations with Burma's military leaders. Burma's smuggling trade with India and Bangladesh is important though less critical, but India's recent role has expanded. Singapore and South Korea are also playing increasingly important roles in trade and arms supply, as has Pakistan in the past. Because of its strategic position and potential wealth, Burma has become the focus of regional power rivalries, especially among China, India, and Thailand.

The United States has diverse interests in Burma, including general humanitarian and human rights interests, a concern with stemming the narcotics flow, and possible investment and trade roles. Foreign aid projects, including antinarcotics activities, have been halted since the 1988 coup, pending improvement in the human rights situation. During the precoup demonstrations, the United States figured prominently because of its support for liberalization and democracy.

The prognosis for Burma is necessarily mixed. Antithetical elements are likely to emerge in mixtures that may be quite logical for

Burma, although puzzling to foreign observers. The gradual departure of Ne Win from the political scene will free the state to make a new set of decisions, but the absence of his cohesive force will raise further issues. The new leadership will likely be dominated by the military, but the emergence of civilians, such as Aung San Suu Kyi, indicates that the future may not be as monolithic as it seemed some years ago.

It is likely that Burma will retain its strong tendencies to factionalism within any new political equation, which will in turn give greater opportunities for nonproductive rent-seeking activities and corruption. It is possible that no single party will win a clear majority in the 1990 elections, making political alliances necessary and creating a government that is essentially weak. Accommodation with the military will be required of any new regime, which will likely be dominated directly by the military until about 1992, and indirectly thereafter. Although a return to military or single-party rule may occur under a dire national emergency, such rule is unlikely to last long except under martial law, the process of formalistic pluralism having proceeded too far for a return to the patterns of the past quarter-century.

A new government will have to make concessions to the minorities, an area that will be carefully watched by the military. Whatever agreement is reached under a new constitution will probably satisfy no single group completely.

The opening to the internal and external private sectors is real and necessary but not without difficulties, for there is a naiveté on the part of the government in dealing with foreign businessmen. The internal danger is that foreigners will once again take over much of the economy, which would lead to nationalistic reactions that might endanger national political and economic development.

The assistance of foreign institutions will be critical for Burma, but these outsiders will strain the cultural tolerance of the state. At the same time, massive foreign aid could vitiate the government's interest in making major, sweeping, and needed reforms.

Ultimately, Burma will need to develop a meritocratic civil service that is capable of handling the increasing complexity of the economy and the nation's growing urban needs. Urbanization will require greatly enhanced employment opportunities in conjunction with an already expanded educational system. This can only come from a revitalized private sector.

Although it is impossible at this stage to predict which individuals will govern Burma, it is likely that, as in the past, a strong leader will emerge. The absolute dichotomies so familiar to Western thinking may have little relevance to analysis of the Burmese situation, which will unfold at a Burmese pace and in a Burmese manner.

I. Background of the 1988 Coup

On September 18, 1988, the Burmese military executed a coup to shore up a government that had virtually collapsed. This was the third military intervention into contemporary Burmese political life. The first two such coups, in 1958 and 1962, had replaced civilian regimes that, in the military's eyes, were failing. This latest, most bloody, action was different; it was the military's way of reasserting control over an urban population in revolution. These citizens had profoundly threatened the quasi-military authorities struggling to maintain power in the face of the most massive public demonstrations in recorded Burmese history. From the viewpoint of the government of the Socialist Republic of the Union of Burma, this was a friendly coup; the active-duty military simply took the place of their former *tatmadaw* (armed forces) colleagues who had years earlier retired to assume government positions. There was thus no governmental resistance.

For the population, however, the coup was devastating. In revolt against political, economic, and social conditions that had become increasingly intolerable, the people had been on the verge of victory; "people power," in the recent Philippine or South Korean sense, seemed about to triumph. But the people were stopped by the massive, unrestrained force of the army, with an incalculable number of deaths. Between March and September 1988 some four thousand to five thousand people almost certainly died, although government figures are only one-tenth of this, while some opposition estimates are twice as high. It was not the Philippines that proved to be the model for Burma; rather Burma provided a preview of China's Tiananmen Square a year later.

The events leading to the coup, the martial law regime that followed, and the present scheduling of elections for May 1990, supposedly to return some civilian government to power, are only explicable in historical context. Foremost is the personal legacy of General Ne Win, followed by the institutional heritage of the civilian (1948–58, 1960–62) and military (1958–60, 1962–) periods.

The Role of Ne Win

Behind all three coups, and indeed orchestrating the critical role of the military since independence in 1948, stands *Bogyoke* (General)

Ne Win. Contemporary Burma cannot be understood without consideration of his influence.

Born in 1911 of Sino-Burman parentage as Shu Maung, Ne Win is now in titular retirement, although he almost certainly influences and indeed is widely believed to control critical decisions. Residing in his isolated home on Inya Lake in Rangoon, he now plays the role of a Burmese Cardinal Richelieu.

Ne Win has been in the limelight since the early 1940s, when he was trained by the Japanese for anti-British activities as one of the "30 Comrades" along with Aung San—the father of Burmese independence, who was assassinated in 1947 and whose memory is perpetuated through portraits in every government office and on some of the currency, and through carefully selected reprints of his writings. Ne Win's close association with Aung San and the latter's continuing legacy have been themes of government propaganda since 1962; Ne Win has been portrayed as having been handed the mantle of leadership from *Bogyoke* Aung San, which gave him popular legitimacy. The advantage of that relationship is now threatened by the emergence of Aung San's daughter, Suu Kyi, as a contender for power.

Ne Win's career illustrates one important strand in Burmese history: critical figures have generally been either of the scholar/monk persuasion or warrior/unifier leaders. As (U) Nu (Burma's prime minister for most of the civilian period) may be considered an example of the former, Ne Win and Aung San are in the latter category. A leading Burmese military officer remarked in 1988 that as King Anawrahta first unified Burma in the 11th century and his son King Kyanzittha solidified the kingdom, so in the 20th century *Bogyoke* Aung San founded independent Burma and *Bogyoke* Ne Win solidified it. The analogy in Burmese eyes is apt and may help to explain both the tenacity with which Ne Win has continuously held authority in Burma and the public's acceptance of his leadership.

Ne Win's role in the preindependence period of the 1940s proved critical to Burma's future. Before independence in 1948, he was commander of the 4th Burma Rifles. In the British tradition of loyalty to one's regiment, he has drawn his closest associates from that unit (that is, Aung Gyi, Tin Pe, San Yu, Sein Lwin, Aye Ko, Kyaw Tin, Tun Tin, Tha Kyaw, and others). As one disgruntled officer remarked, had *he* been in the 4th Burma Rifles, he would have been a government minister already.

From deputy commander of the Burma army upon independence in 1948, Ne Win became army commander a year later, when the Karen chief-of-staff was retired during the insurrection by the

Karen minority. Ne Win also served at various times as minister of defense and deputy prime minister during the first civilian period. His role has always been pivotal.

In 1958 the Burma army took over the civilian government that had been led by Nu. Ne Win became prime minister, and the army was infused into all ministerial, managerial, and economic activities. The 1958 action was a "constitutional coup," a military intervention legitimized by the legislative action of a civilian government that had no other recourse. Burma had been on the verge of civil war as two competing factions of the Anti-Fascist People's Freedom League (AFPFL) organized against each other. Nu led the "Clean AFPFL," and Kyaw Nyein and Ba Swe the "Stable AFPFL." The army was "invited in" constitutionally by Nu. Ne Win became prime minister for what was initially designed to be a six-month period, but which lasted three times as long.

In retrospect, the military's role at that time may have created a model for its actions following its takeover in 1988. In both 1958 and 1988 the army felt a need for quick, decisive, positive action to legitimate its power and demonstrate its efficacy. Troops cleaned the streets, painted the buildings, purged the bureaucracy, moved squatters to the outskirts of Rangoon, exhorted traders to lower prices in the bazaars, and attempted to take quick action against the insurgents in border regions.

In February 1960, free elections were finally held under military auspices. Nu and his reorganized Union Party were returned to power, even though the military was said to have preferred his opponents. The current army has played up this precedent to assure observers of its good faith regarding the elections planned for 1990. The analogy may not hold, however, as so many vital changes have occurred since 1960 and so many problems are now more intractable.

Although there is evidence that some key *tatmadaw* leaders were quickly disillusioned with Nu's return to head a vacillating civilian government in 1960 and wanted to move against it, it was not until March 2, 1962, that the military executed a second coup. Publicly justified as intended to save the nation's unity in the face of ethnic minority dissent and the potential dissolution of the Union, and timed to enable the army to arrest minority leaders assembled in Rangoon for a conference, the coup was perhaps more generally motivated by the army's perceived need for determined leadership (as self-defined)—and by its previous taste of power.

Ne Win now ruled by fiat: first as chair of the Revolutionary Council until 1974; then as chair of the Council of State, and thus the equivalent of president, under the 1974 constitution. More important, Ne Win was chair of the Burma Socialist Programme Party (BSPP), which he founded in 1962 and which was established under the constitution as the leader of the state and its only legitimate political force.

But it was not the position Ne Win held that was important. It was his persona and his power base. His network inspired intense loyalties. Saw Maung later said he regarded Ne Win as a parent; other military leaders indicated that they loved and respected him. All senior military officials owed their promotions to him. Important as well were the dossiers Ne Win kept on all influential people. There was an element of Burmese court intrigue in his operations, and he was treated virtually as a traditional monarch.

When in August 1981 Ne Win announced his retirement as president to ensure a peaceful transition to new leadership, he significantly kept his position as party chair. Most observers at that time felt that as long as Ne Win was alive and well and in the country, his influence would be pervasive. And so it has been.

It is perhaps impossible at this juncture to separate fact from conjecture, but over time Ne Win, although alert and intelligent, seemed to become increasingly mercurial and isolated from reality. His confederates refused to argue with his views, or even to disagree mildly, and they apparently shielded him from many unpleasant facts of Burmese economic and political life. Ne Win was "Number One" or the "Old Man"; even his cabinet would take no action that might upset him and invoke his acerbic wrath. Decisions were postponed pending his change of mood, opportunities lost because of pervasive fear. Belatedly Ne Win would recognize problems, but the hierarchical relationships that initially denied their existence made it impossible to find solutions.

Hierarchy became a solid pattern in Burma's government. Military and party rank provided high status and perquisites. Ne Win was conceptually and Rangoon geographically at the acme, while the people and the periphery were without power, far below. As with so many Burmese political leaders, Ne Win seems to have lacked a strong ideological or intellectual base. Rather, he was influenced—as were so many of the associates of his youth—by vague socialist goals and suspicion of a private sector controlled by foreigners. When asked whether Ne Win was an ideologically committed socialist, one high-ranking officer scoffed, "Ne Win will be a socialist when Mao Zedong learns to play golf." Yet Ne Win used socialism for his own ends, and perhaps as the quickest, most feasible alternative to foreign economic domination.

11

As in earlier Burmese history, no clear line of succession was established. Occasionally, Ne Win indicated an heir apparent: Aung Gyi in 1962; Tin Pe in the later 1960s; San Yu or Tin Oo (former intelligence chief) later. But if the heir became popular or wielded too much influence, he was summarily replaced on some pretext. General Tin Oo, now an opposition leader, said that Ne Win "devoured" those whom he groomed as replacements. It is ironic that the only successor who was legally chosen—San Yu as president and vice chairman of the BSPP—actually left the government along with Ne Win in July 1988. Ne Win seemed unable to share power, not unusual in Burmese history. He is still credited by the public and by many of his associates with an uncanny ability to orchestrate even the most improbable scenarios. Whenever anything inexplicable happened in Burma during the past 26 years, rumors always credited Ne Win as the *deus ex machina*. They still do.

Ne Win's command over daily decisions may now be over, probably at his own request. Nevertheless, his influence on major initiatives and his capacity to veto were critical to events in 1988 and probably continue to be important in this transitional period—although this was denied as recently as July 5, 1989, by General Saw Maung. Significantly, Ne Win was seen publicly for the first time since July 1988 on March 27, 1989, Armed Forces Day, Burma's most important annual military celebration. As Ne Win retires from the limelight, his daughter Sanda is said to have taken up her father's mantle and to protect his interests, often by meeting with critical military figures. As a major in the army medical corps and in her familial role, Sanda is important and highly controversial.

The Heritage of the Union of Burma

Although Ne Win's role in 1988 continued to be pivotal, the recent crisis and its aftermath were not the product of a single man, nor even of the military era in which he was the salient figure. Rather, there is considerable continuity between Burma's earlier era of monarchic power and the civilian and military periods following independence.

The Burmese state, however it was governed in practice, has conceptually always been centrist. In a tradition that began in India, the monarch lived at the symbolic center of the universe, which the capital was designed to represent magically. The monarch was theoretically omnipotent. Whatever power he lacked in practice was made up for by the theory of his glory and his role as an embryonic Buddha or world monarch.

Burma's colonial governors, who defined the country's borders for the first time and executed power horizontally, made centralism more efficient both at the periphery and in the capital. But they also introduced capitalism and foreign domination of an increasingly monetized economy. They exacerbated minority problems and, governing Burma first from Calcutta and then from Delhi, introduced massive Indian immigration at all skill levels. The colonial interlude lasted only 62 years, but it had an enormous impact.

The British provided a system of modern education. They disestablished an old elite; the Burman area was the only Asian colonial region in which the precolonial elites did not return to some form of social, political, or economic power in the postcolonial period. Britain created a new Burmese elite—and inadvertently gave Aung San, Ne Win, Nu, and others the opportunity to gain popularity in the anticolonial struggle.

Atavism has been apparent in both military and civilian governments. Overall, continuity with the Burmese past has been as or even more important than change. Modern leaders have, perhaps unconsciously, continued traditions. Thus when Nu and Ne Win both built pagodas, purified the *sangha*, and corrected Buddhist texts, they were operating in the manner prescribed for the monarchs. When both their governments depended for their survival on the extraction of surpluses from the rice economy, or on their monopolies of teak and oil and their control of the official export trade, they were also acting in the imperial tradition. When governments invoked the traditional term *Hluttaw* (the royal council of the kings) for parliament, and when the image of Saya San (the leader of an anticolonial rebellion exacerbated by the intolerable rural economic conditions of the 1930s) was placed on a new currency note in 1987, these were conscious symbolic reinterpretations of the past.

Effects of Burma's Heritage

Governments in Burma, as elsewhere, operate in a political culture that shapes but does not necessarily dictate policy. Without being deterministic, it is possible to postulate a series of basic attitudes toward government and the economy that have influenced how decisions are reached in Burma, what is considered important when new policies are formulated, and how such attitudes might

13

be overcome, should that be a goal. These attitudes include Burma's tendencies toward political and economic centralization, its concept of personal power and the consequent tendency to factionalism, the saliency of the political process, and the felt need to create a nation with a shared set of goals, rather than simply an internationally recognized state with established boundaries.

When the precolonial pattern of centralized governance was carried into the contemporary era, it proved ill suited to the rising ethnic nationalisms of a multiethnic state, one in which the Burmans have a two-thirds majority but in which various minority groups have struggled for autonomy or, at times, independence. Although Burma's postindependence civilian government gave modest titular authority to the minority areas, power still derived from the capital and its regime, in a modern equivalent of the classic court. That is not to denigrate the complex compromise that was reached in February 1947, before independence, as a result of a historic ethnic meeting at Panglong in the Shan state. Under that and subsequent compromises, the Shan and Kayah states could theoretically secede from the Union by means of a plebiscite to be held after ten years. Power was to be shared. The pre-1962 bicameral legislature had a Chamber of Deputies of 250 and a Chamber of Nationalities of 125, and although the latter had limited authority, it provided an important outlet for minority debate. But the military eliminated this system in the 1962 coup. And in 1974, under a new constitution, the military replaced the federal state with a unitary one, placing power constitutionally under the control of the only legal party, the Burma Socialist Programme Party. Individual minority men and women could theoretically rise in that party and through the army; in fact, few minority men and no women reached anywhere near the personal pinnacle of power. Nor did they have any institutional power or even a political voice. Although the military created seven states for minorities and organized the Burman area into seven divisions (equivalent to provinces), the balance was fictive. Power had in fact been centralized, even when it was theoretically dispersed.

The centralization of political power also affected and was affected by economic policies. State economic planning and socialism had been intellectual hallmarks of Burmese politics. Even before independence, it was assumed that the state would be socialist, and later under Nu's *Pyidawtha*, or "Happy Land," socialist planning, a number of public industries were established without adequate economic rationales, but rather to enhance the regime's political and social image. With this strong heritage, socialism was little ques-

14

tioned when it was stressed in the 1962 coup; at issue was the degree, not the concept, of nationalization. Significantly, when the BSPP Congress considered economic reforms in 1971, socialism was again endorsed, and when it met to determine new measures to encourage the private sector on July 23, 1988, the fundamental socialist basis of the state was reportedly never seriously discussed.

Power in Burma has historically been viewed in personal terms. Throughout recorded Burmese history, loyalty was to the person of the ruler and not to the throne. Allegiance was rarely paid to ideology or abstract ideals, except perhaps to the principles of Theravada Buddhism that pervade Burman society.

As a result, Burma never developed an institutionalized, neutral, and professional civil service (the Confucian bureaucratic model of China, Japan, Korea, Vietnam, and now Singapore), where loyalty was to the principles of service and state. The one exception where such loyalties existed was the Indian, and then Burma, Civil Service, which was introduced under the British and was the most elite (and probably the most competent) bureaucratic element that Burmese society has yet seen. The military forced the last remnants of this group to retire following the coup of 1962. Nu remarked in 1958 that even civil servants had divided loyalties: on the one hand to the party (and its leader); on the other, to their ministry. The military government created a new civil service as an appendage of its party, the BSPP; advancement to middle management required party membership or former military rank (the two were often fused). Even the new military government's September 1988 order that active-duty military and civil servants could not be members of any party did not change either the concept of a personalized civil service or the consequent divided bureaucratic loyalties, if not to a particular party, then to the military itself functioning as if it were a party.

Furthermore, since loyalties are personal, political party leadership is more generally based on entourages rather than ideologies. This is what has made factionalism a key condition of Burmese political life since the preindependence period. Factionalism, although less well understood externally, is probably a key to the military as well. Even when military or political groups were ideologically committed, such as those on the extreme left in the Red and White Flag Communist parties of two generations ago, factionalism was rife and deadly. The inability of opposition leaders in 1988 and 1989 to come together even in the face of an apparent major military-political threat is evidence of factionalism's strong hold. Ne Win's perceived need to eliminate from positions of authority not

15

only all possible claimants to his "throne" but all their followers as well (as in the case of General Tin Oo in 1983), even those at very low levels of authority, demonstrates the strength of these personal loyalties.

Perhaps Ne Win's single greatest asset has been that he has personally been above factional disputes, even if by singling out favorites he created the conditions under which they might flourish. In a sense, all factions centered on him. Some of Ne Win's closest colleagues have created entourages, but Ne Win himself cleverly played one associate off against another. It may be argued that the 4th Burma Rifles was a kind of faction, but it was unique because it was Ne Win's, and Ne Win made it critical to the distribution of power in Burma.

In contemporary Burma, political considerations dominate all public policy measures, economic and social. The economic reforms attempted in 1971 and announced at the first BSPP party congress that year were intended to create more economic rationality in the state sector, providing industries autonomy in hiring, firing, and pricing. The reforms also changed economic priorities within the state to exploitation of Burma's natural resources. But the reforms floundered because of political fears throughout the hierarchy. When Burmese politics became monolithic, economic reforms became virtually impossible unless explicitly mandated from the top.

In such a context, all economic measures are politically motivated. Ne Win's attempt to liberalize the grain trade on September 1, 1987, was foremost a political decision to placate the peasantry, rather than one prompted by economic rationality. Yet it had important economic ramifications.

The final issue for Burmese politics, perhaps the most important, is how to build a nation from disparate ethnic, religious, and linguistic groups. Each Burman government has tried unsuccessfully to deal with two aspects of this problem: the economic power of foreigners—namely Chinese, those from the Indian subcontinent, and Europeans; and the role of indigenous minorities.

Both these problems can be traced to the colonial period, in which the British first encouraged foreign (especially Indian) immigration and then governed separately from Burma Proper most of the minority peoples in the frontier regions. The traditional regimes in Burma were more concerned with royal—that is, state—power and glory, and with increasing population in an underpopulated region, than with ethnic distinctions, and Burman attitudes toward most tribal minorities were clearly condescending.

16

The economic power of the Europeans was vastly circumscribed after independence and eliminated altogether after 1962. Indian (including Bengali) economic power was effectively truncated with the virtual expulsion of some two hundred thousand people at about the same time. Chinese economic power has recently grown. A 1982 law effectively provided second-class citizenship ("associate citizenship") to those from groups who had not resided in Burma prior to the First Anglo-Burmese War of 1824–26 and who could not prove under highly complex conditions the Burmese birth of their grandparents. This law allowed such individuals to engage in certain businesses, but not to hold official positions of trust in the government or the military. A more equitable distribution of internal economic power is vital to the economic success and legitimacy of any future government.

Of even greater importance is the problem of the indigenous minorities and their access to political and economic power. Some scholars maintain that Western historians have exaggerated the role of ethnicity in Burmese history, indeed have even created the notion that such a role exists. Yet as Burman nationalism has grown in the 20th century, so has other ethnic nationalism. Whatever the appropriate traditional solutions to this problem, they no longer seem relevant in the contemporary world. The minorities on Burma's periphery have been in closer contact with the outside world since 1962 than the Burmans because of their geographic locations and their external economic links. In the 1950s Burma averaged about 92,000 visitors annually; after the 1962 coup, the figure dropped to about 15,000. In 1987, visitors to Burma were 1 percent of those to Thailand.

The minorities seem to have been more receptive than the Burmans to Western institutions, religions, and ideas. The reasons for this are unclear, for although weaker cultural or social systems, or missionary influence, may have played some part, these factors do not explain the receptivity of the Shan and other Buddhist minorities.

The Burman population is the only major ethnic group that has no traditional ethnic cohorts in some other country (although modern exiles abound). The Shan are closely related to the Thai and Lao; Karen and Mon straddle the Thai-Burmese border; there are more Kachin in China than in Burma; Chin and Naga are on both sides of the India-Burma frontier; and many of the Arakanese Muslims are closely related to the Bengalis. This complex pattern of cultures and loyalties remains an unresolved heritage to which any new government will have to pay special attention.

Thus the government has been looking for the elixir that would turn Burma from a state into a nation, with a common, constructed ideology, such as Pancasila in Indonesia; or a common symbol of national unity, such as the Thai monarch and his role as defender of the Buddhist faith; or even, as in the case of South Korea, a common enemy (i.e., North Korea). Burma has lacked such symbols, for whenever one is chosen, some group is threatened. Nu's espousal of Buddhism as the state religion in 1960 caused furors among non-Buddhist minorities as well as in the Burman military. Ne Win's efforts to provide a secular, unifying ideology, "The Burmese Way to Socialism," offended few, but failed through incompetence. It is significant that in each period, national unity has been a persistent theme in the names of parties (Nu's United Party, the National Unity Party of 1988, the Karen National Union, and so forth), in the slogans of the military, and in the platforms of most of the political parties of 1988–89. Any new government is also likely to seek some overarching theme that will unite Burma's diverse peoples in a common nation-building task. The military regime has attempted to use the *tatmadaw* in such a manner, but with what success is as yet unclear. As we have seen, economic liberalism and political pluralism have inherent difficulties if either or both are to become such symbols. Xenophobia is a distinct but potentially harmful possibility as well.

All these factors—the personal nature of power, a high degree of centralism, and a lack of national unity—influenced the traumatic events of 1988, to which we will now turn.

II. Precipitating Causes of the 1988 Coup

The cumulative weight on the urban populace of two-and-a-half decades of political frustration and economic mismanagement was exacerbated by the excesses of 1988. These excesses were perpetrated first by the riot police (*lon htein*) and then by the military. The civilian reaction in urban areas was both swift and massive, and sometimes brutal, as general social anomie exploded first into demonstrations and then into violence.

Although the causes of this reaction were internal, there is evidence from banners and posters that the mass, articulated need for political liberalization had been encouraged by events in a number of Asian societies. Urban Burmese were aware of liberalizing movements in other countries, such as the Philippines and South Korea, and the international press, if not the Burmese, expected Burma to be next.

Burma in 1988 was in the midst of an urban revolution that started with the students, then became multiclass and ubiquitous. Its suppression with great violence may be likened to that of the Paris Commune of 1871 and that of Tiananmen Square in June 1989.

The military, together with some members of the old elite, seem to have become increasingly fearful that the elaborately constructed power fabric of the society was becoming undone and that anarchy or leftist elements might eventually prevail. The timing of the September 18 coup, however, probably reflected internal incidents that gave rise to fears of deteriorating military discipline and a consequent collapse of state power.

The volatile nature of Burmese cities in 1988 must be compared with the relative quiescence of the previous 26 years of Ne Win's rule, for although there had been demonstrations and killings—most prominently in 1962, 1967, and 1974—they were of a different kind and magnitude. Previous uprisings had been limited to specific groups—students, monks, and others; although some were extensive, they were not ubiquitous. The population as a whole had not risen up in protest. The level of violence had never before reached that of Thailand in 1973, for example, or of Sri Lanka in the 1980s, both of which are also Theravada Buddhist societies. Evidently, by 1988 Burma had undergone changes that had influenced the magnitude and depth of popular resentment. These were both economic and political.

19

The Economic Malaise

On December 11, 1987, the United Nations General Assembly declared that Burma was a "least developed nation," with annual incomes below US$200 per capita and a low level of industrial development and literacy. Burma was named one of ten countries (including Chad, Ethiopia, Nepal, and Bangladesh) where economic conditions were so bad and poverty so widespread that there seemed little hope for development. These nations seemed doomed to exist on continuous handouts of foreign aid.

Some observers argued that this categorization was not an accurate portrait of Burma, where traditionally literacy was high (the highest between Suez and Japan in the 19th century, so travelers noted) and where the extensive black market was ignored in official statistics. But the Burmese government had long campaigned for that designation so that it would receive more grant assistance and lower interest rates on loans, thus alleviating its mushrooming international debt. That it intentionally withheld knowledge of this newly acquired status from its people for four months, and then only mentioned it in conjunction with positive (and erroneous) stories on Burmese economic accomplishments, indicates the government's recognition of the stigma that the educated Burmese public would attach to such a designation.

Some Burmese noted that in the mid-1950s, Burma, Thailand, and South Korea had close to the same populations and all had per capita incomes well below US$100 per year. Yet it was Burma that was the most richly endowed with natural resources. In fact, Burma may have been unique among developing states in that it was an exporter of both energy (oil) and food—the largest rice exporter (3.1 million tons in 1940–41) in the world before World War II. By 1988–89, official Thai per capita income was 4 times the Burmese figure of US$200, and South Korean income was almost 20 times that much, despite Korea's shortage of natural resources. Twenty-five years ago, more than 40 percent of the Korean population was below the poverty line; today that figure is less than 10 percent. In Burma, on the other hand, long noted as a land without hunger and a mecca for Indians and Chinese seeking economic advancement, over 40 percent of the population had fallen into poverty by the mid-1980s. The Burmese standard of living in the 1970s was probably still below pre–World War II levels, and it is not much higher today. Evidently, the political economy of Burma had failed—and needlessly.

Ne Win occasionally recognized this failure. He articulated these problems first in 1967, then in 1971, and most recently in 1987. In

20

August 1987, in a speech at the BSPP congress, he stated that Burma was in difficult straits and that economic, political, and even constitutional changes were needed. He urged that party members make suggestions for improvements to be presented at the party congress scheduled for the summer of 1989.

But Ne Win did not wait for suggestions. The next month he initiated two moves with critical economic consequences. They were in fact antithetical to each other in important respects.

On September 1, 1987, Ne Win announced the most sweeping economic liberalization program that Burma had seen since the military coup of March 2, 1962. Nine grains, most notably rice, were freed from the government market. Previously, paddy (unmilled rice) had to be sold to the state at fixed, low prices. Both the monarchical and modern Burmese governments had extracted the considerable difference between the state purchase price and the export and consumer sales price and used it to support the state apparatus. Now farmers were free to buy and sell at free-market rates to whomever they wished.

The immediate effect of this move was to raise farm income. It may also have been intended to raise production through better incentives, which had been marginal, but the change was instituted too far into the growing season to have any effect on production in 1987.

In February 1988 the government also allowed the private export of rice, but because traders could not hold foreign currencies and because the exchange rate was some seven times overvalued, such legal, private exports did not take place. The government could continue its export ventures because its priority was acquiring foreign exchange, even if it lost money in kyat. The state could always print more local currency; private traders did not have that luxury.

Although this liberalization was touted as an economic reform, it depleted government income in the short run and was only marginally effective without other economic measures, which were not forthcoming. Liberalization was, however, an astute short-term political move. The bulk of the population was rural, and the move seemed to placate the peasantry.

But on September 5, 1987, just days after the grain liberalization measures, Ne Win dropped his second bombshell, which contradicted his first effort. This second plan was said to have been personally determined, with the party's Central Executive Committee ordered to vote approval without debate. This second plan may have been the most massive demonetization in the contemporary

21

world. All bank notes above US$2.50 at the legal rate of exchange (these were notes of K15, K25, and K75) were simply declared to be illegal, with no recompense to be given for them. Immediately, almost 70 percent of the currency in circulation was invalid.

This affected the whole population, with immediate results. Students demonstrated, so schools were ordered closed to prevent disturbances. The government provided some students who were without funds with K100 so that they would return to their villages or towns. There were rumors that some military officers had bought at huge discounts or had commandeered newly illegal currency, which was then surreptitiously converted to legal bills for personal use.

The purpose of the demonetization, according to the government, was to eliminate the black market and the smuggling trade. The state, in fact, depended on this trade to sustain an economy that could no longer produce enough to meet essential needs. Some critics also claimed that the government had been printing so much money to finance its internal debt that this was merely a quick means to cut the money supply and thus curb inflation, which had been growing rapidly. Other observers claimed that abstruse astrological and numerological calculations (all involving the number nine or numbers adding up to nine) were involved, designed to enable Ne Win (for whom the number nine is said to be lucky) to live to be 90 years old. Whether or not this is accurate, it is significant that it was widely believed, indicating both the continuing aura around Ne Win's person and the seemingly vast capacity for the personalization of power in Burmese society.

This demonetization was the third since the 1962 coup. The first, in the early 1960s, had been directed against the foreign business community. The second, in 1985, was also ostensibly directed against the black market. In those earlier cases, however, if holders of the newly illegal notes could demonstrate that they had been legally obtained (whatever in fact was the case), they were allowed within limits to keep them. This was not permitted in the third demonetization.

The effect on Burmese society was electric. People also feared future demonetizations. Businesses, believing that a future demonetization would be scheduled on a weekend, brought sealed bags of currency notes to the banks on Friday afternoons, where for a small bribe they were accepted without being counted by the banks' insufficient staffs. If there had been a demonetization, these businesses would have been credited with bank deposits; otherwise, they would withdraw their sacks of currency Monday morning.

When less than a year later the state advocated the resuscitation of the private sector, it had already eliminated much of the legal capital that might have been invested in it. For the citizenry, however, there were other possibilities. No one wished to hold cash, so urban dwellers bought up any commodity (including land—urban land in Rangoon brought K10 million per acre, Mandalay land K20 million because it was closer to the Chinese trade), thus fueling both inflation and the smuggling trade. Gold was also in demand; some say that even the increase in opium production may have been partly attributable to the need for tradable commodities. Peasants held onto their paddy. The result was that the price of rice skyrocketed, and by the late spring of 1988 it was three times its previous level. There was also no rice for legal exports.

At the same time, the macroeconomic picture was at its nadir. External debt had risen to more than US$5 billion (or about 70 percent of GNP), both because of excessive borrowing and because of the appreciation of the Japanese yen—Japan was Burma's largest creditor—and the deutsche mark—West Germany was Burma's second largest bilateral lender. The debt-service ratio was, according to various calculations, between 75 and 91 percent. In 1955 Burma's debt was US$62.3 million, in 1975, US$319.9 million, but by 1984 it had risen to US$3.4 billion.

Internal debt rose as well; the State Economic Enterprises (SEEs) —the public sector—were borrowing heavily from the government (their annual debt was K4.3 billion in 1984–85). The government had to cut legal imports. These had reached K6.3 billion in 1982–83 but were reduced to K3.9 billion by 1987–88, while exports that year fell to K2.4 billion, 25 percent below the 1982–83 level. Because of the shortage of foreign exchange, which had dropped to about US$29 million by December 1987, Burma could import neither raw materials nor spare parts for its factories. Production and capacity utilization fell as debt rose. The interest on one glass factory's debt alone was more than the factory's total national sales.

In contrast, in the late 1970s and early 1980s macroeconomic growth appeared encouraging, but the figures were misleading (Ne Win later admitted they had been inflated without his knowledge—to please the "Old Man"). In fact, growth had been led by increased rice production, but had then reached a plateau because of limited water availability (only 12 to 13 percent of farmed land was irrigated, mostly as insurance against a failed monsoon rather than for double cropping) and shortages of fertilizer, a large percentage of which had to be imported. Oil production, which the state had anticipated to be three times actual production, had in fact fallen to prewar levels, only about one-third of internal requirements. Government figures for oil production at its peak were 34,000 barrels daily; by 1989 it was 15,000 barrels. Diesel fuel was in short supply, slowing the development projects financed by foreign aid. Kerosene was no longer produced, forcing greater use of charcoal, and thus forest degradation. Coupled with longer-term economic issues, the economic stage was set for confrontation.

At the same time, the Japanese government made a major departure from precedent in its foreign aid programs. As the largest bilateral donor, in 1987 holding about US$2 billion in outstanding debt, it reversed policy. In April 1988 it warned the Burmese deputy prime minister that unless Burma made substantive (but unspecified) economic reforms, Japan would have to reconsider its economic support. The relationship between Burma and Japan had been long and close, reflecting Burma's reliance on Japanese war reparations and then economic aid. This *volte-face* probably had a considerable impact on the economic liberalization that was announced later that year.

Political Frustration

Institutionalized political debate in modern Burma has a history of some fifty years. Under the British in the 1930s, when Burma became separated from India, political parties mushroomed. Although these groups merely served the ends of individual leaders, they did establish the precedent of a multiparty system that survived until 1962. Even though Burma had been led by the all-encompassing Anti-Fascist Peoples Freedom League, parties and organizations inside and outside of that grouping were vigorous, and their debates were reported in a relatively open press. Whether the term "democracy" can be appropriately applied during those periods is debatable, but political pluralism was certainly in evidence.

Some scholars argue that this period was an anomaly in Burmese history, that it did not reflect tradition or established concepts of the use of power and the role of the state. Although this may be true in part, and although many elder Burmese remember many frustrating elements of multiparty politics, some nostalgia for that less-constrained period (if not for its now elderly leadership) was generated by the sweeping changes taking place from 1986 in other

24

Asian societies, and in some of the communist states as well. Politically and economically, Burma appeared to have been left behind.

Although the military caretaker government had generally been welcomed in 1958, it was viewed, and viewed itself, as a transitory stage in Burmese political life. Following the coup of 1962, however, the single-party system seemed permanent, insofar as permanency was possible within the Buddhist concept of the impermanence of all things, a concept embodied in the state ideology. The role of the party as leader of the state was codified in the constitution of 1974, along the lines of an East European model.

The BSPP continued to expand its membership, moving from its initial phase as a cadre party of some two dozen military leaders in 1962 to a mass party that held its first congress in 1971. Nevertheless, the military retained its control of this political mobilization. This it accomplished by having some two-thirds of the approximately 160,000 military (at the time) at the party's core; by encouraging retired military and police to join; and by controlling the formation and membership of ancillary organizations, including peasant and workers' groups, party youth leagues (whose memberships all numbered in the millions), and state and cooperative shops and groupings. There was hardly a family in Burma that was not tied in some manner to the BSPP, which also had responsibility for local administration. It was the party that theoretically had the power, for example, to pass on the transfer of usufruct rights to rural land from parent to child, or to certify that a woman could have an abortion. The party controlled the press, which had been nationalized. Foreign influences of any sort were held to a minimum.

With the increase in the party's power under military guidance, there developed an administration that rewarded party loyalty over competence. Examinations for entry into the civil service came to be devoted to assessing political conformity, not technical capacity. Promotions required party membership. This resulted in decisions made on the basis of party and political considerations, not on the merits of an issue. Each lower level looked to the higher party level for approval or to avoid punishment. The cabinet itself looked to Ne Win. By the mid-1970s the party structure was rigid and unresponsive to needs external to its own organization. As a result, government administration suffered.

Since the state controlled both the political and economic processes, the political structure was blamed for shortages and high prices; for rigidity of management; for favoritism in decisions; and for the policy of rewarding not only the party faithful but also their children with perquisites that perpetuated their high status.

There were some, especially students, who sought political pluralism after the 1962 coup. Students drew on an illustrious heritage of student anticolonial activism from the 1930s—and most of the leaders of the first two decades of independent rule (including Ne Win, Nu, and Aung Gyi) had had roles in that earlier process. When the Ne Win government responded to student riots and the large, officially unrecognized number of student deaths by ordering the destruction of the Rangoon University student union building on July 7, 1962, this was an ironic break with its own past. This building had been the site of much of the earlier student ferment of the 1930s as well as of opposition to Ne Win's new military government. When President Maung Maung offered to rebuild it in September 1988, he was symbolically recognizing students' continuing importance in Burmese political ferment.

This ferment went beyond students to all youth, for the role of younger monks and new entrants into the labor market was also critical. Yet increasingly, young people were viewed as economically marginal by an unresponsive government, and they themselves had little hope for their own future. The 1974 death of former U.N. Secretary-General (U) Thant, Burma's most internationally illustrious son, created an opportunity for antigovernment youth protest. Thant had been a close associate of Nu, in fact his secretary, and had he been in Rangoon at the time of the 1962 coup, he most likely would have been arrested along with Nu. The government attempted to downgrade both his funeral and burial site. Students seized the body, first took it to Rangoon University and demanded a proper funeral, then rallied around the Shwedagon Pagoda, and finally were dispersed by the military with large, uncounted casualties (some say in the hundreds, even thousands). Antigovernment slogans were a prominent element of those demonstrations.

Growing gratuitous government violence against youth contributed to the political frustration, which finally exploded in March 1988. That the precipitating incident of this latest, most deadly round of political turmoil was in fact apolitical indicates the extent of social anxiety and frustration. On March 12, students from the Rangoon Institute of Technology got into a fight with a local teashop proprietor and his patrons, supposedly over the music that was being played in the shop. Violence ensued, one student died, and the riot police were called in under the command of General Sein Lwin (who had also been responsible for the student deaths in 1962 and 1974). The riot police, the *lon htein*, were said to represent a lower element in the increasingly stratified Burmese society; the students were the sons and daughters of the (often military) elite.

These police may have looked with envy at the scions of the privileged. Students were beaten and killed; female students were mishandled and, some say, raped. The riots soon spread to downtown Rangoon. There were many deaths, and a large number of young persons were packed inside a police van to be taken to jail; 41 suffocated in the Burmese equivalent of the Black Hole of Calcutta. It was only in July after an official inquiry that the government admitted these events.

Schools were immediately closed, not to reopen until May 30. Rumors continued to spread. The suffocations in particular were well known, if not admitted by the government. At the same time, the economic hardships increased as rice prices tripled. In early June, students returned to determine who had been killed, arrested, or was still missing. Pressures on the government grew, and by June 16 the situation once more became explosive. The student demonstrations again spread to downtown Rangoon, where many others joined in. By June 21, the military had opened fire on the crowds, killing a large but unknown number. The universities were once again closed, and a dusk-to-dawn curfew was imposed on Rangoon.

Ne Win went abroad with a large entourage after the March rioting. On his return, it is said that he was appalled to learn of the suffocations. He may have concluded that the economic and political conditions were sufficiently dire to speed up his timetable for change. On July 7, he called for an extraordinary party congress to be held on July 23, to consider economic, political, and constitutional issues. But this was not enough to mollify the country. Although the curfew was lifted in Rangoon two days later, rioting broke out in Taunggyi and in Prome, where martial law was invoked. These disturbances were said to be linked to local, communal Muslim issues, but such problems had often surfaced in previous times of turmoil and were sometimes used by the state to redirect anger onto third parties.

At the July 23 party congress, Ne Win offered his resignation and those of his four closest military associates from party and state positions and from the party itself. He also called for a referendum on whether a multiparty political system should be introduced, with the necessary changes in the constitution. Some say Ne Win had become disillusioned with the party and that he wanted it to be restructured. Others say his move was only a means to transfer responsibility for failure from himself onto the party.

The resignations of Ne Win and his four colleagues from party and state positions were accepted, but they were not allowed to re-

27

sign from the party itself, for party rules made such resignations illegal. The party congress debated whether political pluralism should come to Burma. As the congress continued, it became evident that party stalwarts were not about to relinquish their own authority. Before the vote against the multiparty system and for the continuation of their own untrammeled power, Ne Win, secluded in his home, was said to have been consulted by messenger and to have accepted this conclusion. Perhaps he did not do so reluctantly, for now the party would be responsible for any future failures, rather than Ne Win himself.

The party did approve a wide-ranging reform of the economic system within the existing Burmese framework. These economic measures were also said to have been approved by Ne Win. Significantly, the socialist basis of the state was not questioned. The state was to retain a monopoly on onshore oil production, teak, gems, communications, and the banking sectors, although the private sector was to be encouraged elsewhere. Private foreign firms now could work with public, cooperative, or private organizations, whereas since 1971 they had been limited to relations with the state sector. (In fact, there had only been one foreign firm involved in Burma since 1971, Fritz Werner Industrie-Ausrustungen, 88 percent of whose shares were controlled by the West German government. The company had long, close personal associations with Ne Win and was concerned with armaments, which Ne Win controlled.) The party's Central Executive Committee was given the task of working out the details of the new openness.

In a move that shocked the populace, General Sein Lwin was chosen first as party chair and then, by the *Pyithu Hluttaw* (People's Assembly) as chair of the Council of State, and thus president of the country. The students had wanted him arrested, not promoted. Sein Lwin's elevation could not have taken place without Ne Win's approval. Whatever the internal party logic of this move, it was a major tactical error, suggesting that the party either could not gauge public sentiment or had an inflated concept of its own ability to prevail.

The results were swift and predictable. Students almost immediately began demonstrations at the Shwedagon Pagoda as Sein Lwin jailed Brigadier Aung Gyi and ten of his associates. By August 3 martial law had been declared in Rangoon, and the situation was out of hand nationally as well. During the next month demonstrations spread to some two hundred fifty urban centers. Rice prices rose immediately from their already unprecedented levels, and there were charges of looting. The demonstrations became massive:

28

at their peak more than one million people demonstrated in Rangoon in a single day, and over half a million in Mandalay. Demonstrations of more than one hundred thousand people were commonplace.

August 8 was a critical day. It had great symbolic significance to many Burmese: 8-8-88, "four eights," was the equivalent of the year 888 in the Burmese era, which was the date of the fall of the Ava dynasty (1527 A.D.). A massive strike broke out in Rangoon, followed by demonstrations. All the schools in the country, including primary schools, were closed the following day. Over the next five days throughout the country some three thousand people were killed by the military with unprecedented brutality.

On August 12, the BSPP Central Executive Committee prompted the resignation of Sein Lwin with Ne Win's approval. The taut fabric of the state had begun to unravel. Illegal publications sprang up, and even the government press became openly critical of the administration. Groups such as the All-Burma Bar Council criticized the government. The Rangoon economic professors' association could see in print its statement that the government had misled the people with false economic data, fostered inappropriate policies, and neglected foreign advice, and that state materials could not be trusted. There were the beginnings of a "Rangoon Spring."

On August 19, the day after the army's party cadre met, the BSPP chose Maung Maung, a civilian and the closest nonmilitary associate of Ne Win, as party chair. The *Pyithu Hluttaw* then confirmed him as president. Once a respected legal scholar, Maung Maung had become an apologist for the party and its system and the hagiographer of Ne Win. As a moderate, he might have prevented revolution had he been chosen before Sein Lwin, but it was now too late. Momentum had built up for restructuring of the political and economic system. Demonstrations continued, and indeed their magnitude increased. Calls for a multiparty political system became insistent.

Maung Maung made conciliatory gestures. He suggested a plebiscite on a new political system—but many people said that the demonstrations were in fact such a vote. He also offered to rebuild the Rangoon University student union building. But the liberalization process seemed to build of its own momentum despite Maung Maung's efforts to contain it. The world press reported more extensively on Burma that summer than in the whole history of the state, even though few correspondents were actually in Burma; most reporting was done from Bangkok with telephone calls to

29

Rangoon-based foreign diplomats and nongovernmental figures. The U.S. Senate and House of Representatives passed separate resolutions on Burmese democracy. The Burmese listened to the BBC, Voice of America, and All-India Radio. Since there were few foreign reporters in Burma, events could not be verified, and no doubt mistakes in reporting were made. But the international isolation of Burma was definitely over; it could only be reimposed with great difficulty, perhaps only for short periods under any government.

Local administration broke down and was replaced by ad hoc village or urban ward groups, which often drew upon monks and other respected citizens to keep local order. Although demonstrations included spontaneous outbursts of emotion, they were also well organized, with student leaders illustrating for the most part a sense of responsibility in their crowd control.

As emotional intensity grew, rumors were rife. Military intelligence staff were said to have acted as *agents provocateurs*; the government was rumored to have opened the jails; many attributed orders for killings or other atrocities to Ne Win or his daughter. The pent-up violence of the military was vented in numerous shootings; the people responded with explosive rage—in Rangoon alone there were said to be 54 separate beheadings of suspected government spies (the government later said that 73 persons had been killed by the people).

There were so many calls for an interim government to supervise multiparty elections that the government finally recognized that a plebiscite was not required. Opposition leaders began to emerge. Prominent were Nu, the former prime minister deposed by Ne Win in 1962 and now in his eighties; Aung Gyi, one of Ne Win's earlier heirs apparent, now in his seventies; General Tin Oo, a favorite of Ne Win in the 1970s who later became too popular and was jailed for prior knowledge of an attempted coup against Ne Win in 1976; and Aung San Suu Kyi, the daughter of General Aung San, who was married to an English academic and normally resided in Oxford, but who was now ministering to her dying mother in Rangoon.

As the economic hardships increased, looting spread; some believe it was intensified by the military for their own profit and to blame the opposition. The newspapers eventually reported some 55 significant cases, and the government later reported that 45 factories, 60 godowns (warehouses), 75 office buildings, 22 shops, and other facilities had been destroyed. The government had apparently lost control over urban areas. Foreign embassies and eco-

30

nomic-aid organizations began to evacuate dependents and unessential staff as anarchy seemed to engulf the state. Although foreigners were not threatened, there was fear of chaos as demonstrators marched by the U.S. Embassy, both because of its location on the central square of Rangoon and because the U.S. government was viewed as supportive of political pluralism.

By September it had become evident that the government could no longer control the state. Political parties had been formed, opposition groups illegally constituted. The demonstrations had continued, and all classes and groups, including some from the civil service, the lower echelons of the military, and the party itself, had joined in the antigovernment, prodemocracy marches.

Two incidents were pivotal. On September 15, the crowds at the Ministry of Defense were on the verge of taking over the headquarters, which might have meant the end of the regime. Some say the troops were ready to fire on the crowd. The people were addressed by Brigadier Aung Gyi, who urged them to trust the army and told them that an interim government was being formed. Aung Gyi was successful, and the crowds dispersed. Thus perhaps the single clearest opportunity for success of this revolution was lost. Aung Gyi is still blamed by many for this action.

On September 16, crowds surrounded the Ministry of Trade building, in which some three dozen troops were holed up, said to be fully armed and with sufficient ammunition. It is unclear whether these troops became demoralized and surrendered to the students, who smuggled them out through an angry crowd demanding their heads; or whether, as the government maintains, they were ordered not to shoot. Although some military personnel had previously joined the demonstrations, by now the military regarded the popular uprisings as the ultimate danger to the state, the most palpable sign of the disintegration of the armed forces.

The situation was thus desperate. Anecdotal evidence attests that General Saw Maung, commander in chief of the armed forces, visited Ne Win's residence late on the night of September 17 and again early the next morning. Maung Maung also called on Ne Win at about 3:00 P.M. on September 18. Shortly thereafter, before 4:00 P.M., the military coup took place.

The government claims that the military, mostly from the 22nd Light Infantry Battalion, had been instructed to put a stop to looting, and that those killed were so engaged. A more widespread belief is that the government sought out youth and demonstrators and engaged in wanton acts of violence against a population armed only with jinglees—bicycle spokes on slingshots. In either case, the result was a huge loss of life. Many claim that the majority of the troops brought in had few loyalties to the Rangoon population and that the violence was therefore increased.

Fear and quiet descended on Rangoon and other urban areas. The military established the State Law and Order Restoration Council (SLORC), composed of 19 senior military officers. A new cabinet was formed, with General Saw Maung as its head, and with a sole civilian. The military, which had operated behind the scenes and in mufti, now assumed full, visible, and official command under martial law.

III. Aftermath of the Coup

Immediately following the 1988 coup, Burma seemed to slip off the world information map. The military government (the SLORC) appeared to be intent on isolating Burma once again. Visas for tourists and reporters were denied, and Burmese were not allowed to leave the country. The level of information on Burma reverted to that of the 1960s—sparse, controlled, and highly colored. Reporting came primarily from the border regions, to which dissident students and others had fled and to which the foreign press had access. Foreign reporters also relied on expatriate Burmese. The Burmese press seemed even more tightly controlled and of even poorer quality than in the worst days of the 1960s.

At the same time, the mood of the populace was radically different from only a few months before. Aside from a relatively small number of students who organized underground, the former demonstrators seemed stunned—cowed and fearful. That the situation had just been revolutionary was almost inconceivable.

As the martial law regime continued, however, there was evidence of change. Political parties were registered, criticisms of the state were voiced, and illegal opposition rallies—some fleeting "hit-and-run" affairs, others involving thousands—were staged. It became easier to get passports and leave the country, and many younger, educated Burmese began to do so; the state allowed such departures as a safety valve for boiling emotions. Slowly, planning for an insecure future began. The government and opposition groups were both organizing, each testing how far it could go and the extent to which its opponents would react. Some opposition groups, especially Aung San Suu Kyi and Tin Oo's party, campaigned and held large gatherings in defiance of martial law. The military made shows of force, conspicuously reinforcing its presence in order to intimidate. It seems likely that the military's continuing suppression was further strengthened by the June 1989 events in China. Had the Chinese students succeeded, their victory would probably have encouraged the Burmese students to repeat that success. In any case, by July 1989 the situation had again become more tense.

The Government

The new military government had four fundamental objectives: the reassertion of state (military) control; reform to avoid too close a public identification with the previous government (which in fact it was indirectly supporting); the establishment of internal and external legitimacy; and the amelioration of the country's short-term economic crisis. The new regime began moving toward these goals under martial rule that at the end of 1989 still continues. Although to the outside world the SLORC seems united, to insiders there appear to be differences among its leaders on press treatment, external relations, elections, and internal dissent—differences that might prove important in the future. For example, the SLORC first excluded the press, then invited foreign journalists into the country, and once again in early July 1989 excluded them because of "adverse publicity," actions that may have represented the views of different factions. It is also likely that there have been internal differences on whether, how, and when to hold an election. There remains the question of Ne Win's behind-the-scenes role in these major decisions.

On July 5, 1989, General Saw Maung went to considerable lengths to deny the existence of any divisions within the SLORC, indicating that discussion of policies always resulted in unanimity, and that he and not Ne Win was in charge.

The issue of divisions within the military is of more significance. The lengths to which the *tatmadaw* have gone to deny any divisions indicate heightened military sensitivity to the danger. SLORC Notification 8/88 of October 10, 1988, specifies that "organizational activities, speeches, propaganda, and subversive literature aimed at dividing the Defense Forces are prohibited." This and the edict proclaiming martial law are the two most often mentioned SLORC regulations. On Armed Forces Day, March 27, 1989, Saw Maung maintained that military forces had three essential tasks: providing for national defense and security; preserving law and order and holding elections; and maintaining the unity of the *tatmadaw*. He further indicated that "it is in accord with the 'law of nature' that the indigenous people have love and respect for the *tatmadaw*."

The opposition, most specifically Aung San Suu Kyi, has been accused of fomenting disunity among the armed forces. Given past problems of factionalism and the pressures under which the military must now operate, the specter of splits within the military is real, and one of the major areas to be watched.

Reasserting State Control

During the revolution, authority at the local level seemed to pass to civic leaders and local groups, who attempted to retain some semblance of order, but over whom state authority had been removed. The BSPP, which was supposed to control local government, had collapsed, and in some areas the homes of its staff had even been looted in protest against the party's blatant corruption. Some local party dignitaries were in hiding. So after the coup, the government's first effort was to reestablish a central administration, with a new, competent image.

The state was also renamed, reverting to its original appellation—the Union of Burma. The Burma Socialist Programme Party was scrapped and replaced by the progovernment National Unity Party (NUP), which was then (at least publicly) denied government funding. No active-duty military personnel or civil servants were allowed to join any party, in order to provide the image of neutrality. Those elements of the constitution of 1974 that asserted party leadership over the state were simply ignored; but there was no longer a legal means to amend the constitution, since the *Pyithu Hluttaw* had been abolished. Political indoctrination in the BSPP canons, *The Burmese Way to Socialism* and *The System of Correlation of Man and His Environment*, ceased, and the Political Science Institute, site of much of this training, was quiescent. The People's Justices (untrained party workers, supplemented by advisory lawyers who operated a state-controlled legal system) were eliminated, and the old Supreme Court of the 1947 Constitution, which had been abolished by Ne Win after the coup of 1962, was reestablished. Trained lawyers were now back in charge of the justice system.

Civil servants were forced back to work and given deadlines by which to report to or lose their jobs. Since no other jobs were available, most of them complied. Those who returned were forced to sign confessions of their involvement in the demonstrations or in any other acts determined to be disloyal or detrimental to the state.

During the demonstrations, military intelligence agents had surreptitiously photographed demonstration leaders. Now, house-to-house searches were carried out to find these individuals. Many who were arrested are said to have permanently disappeared. As soon as the coup took place and repression set in, some ten thousand students fled to the borders, most of them east to Thailand. Some joined the ethnic insurgents along the border to receive weapons training in order to return to fight against the military; some moved quietly into Thailand and found employment, as so many tens of thousands had done since 1962. All schools remained

35

closed. It was only in June 1989 that primary schools reopened. In August 1989 middle schools and teacher training institutions reopened. High schools opened at the end of September 1989, medical and dental institutes, vocational schools, and schools of education in October 1989, but other institutions of higher education remained closed. Since 1962, over half-a-dozen years of schooling have been lost through government closures due to anxiety over student demonstrations—a testament both to the perceived power of student activism and to government fears.

Reform and Legitimization

The SLORC attempted to establish a new aura of reform, but in fact it continued many earlier military policies. The military did all that the army had done in 1958 in creating the caretaker government, and then some. It called itself "transitional," it cleaned the streets and whitewashed the buildings, it moved squatters out of Rangoon to the distant suburbs, increased activities against the insurgencies, and exhorted traders to lower prices in the bazaars. It established welfare centers, where rice was sold to the general public in limited quantities at below-market prices to ease the urban economic burden, which had worsened significantly. The military also promised multiparty elections at some indefinite date, which in early 1989 was determined to be May 1990 and later announced as May 27. It promulgated a draft election law on March 1, 1989, and a final one on June 1. On April 1, 1989, it announced the reorganization of the state economic enterprises.

The precoup leadership was carefully screened from public view, although its members were not put under arrest or in any way harassed. Some were even used productively. While Sein Lwin remained hidden, Maung Maung was said to be helping the government draft new legislation, and Aye Ko to be advising the administration. High-level officials like General Saw Maung and General Khin Nyunt, chief of intelligence, were rumored to visit Ne Win regularly. Finally, on Armed Forces Day (March 27, 1989), Ne Win publicly appeared for the first time since July 1988. The populace had not doubted his continuing influence in the interim, but the military evidently felt in firm enough control to allow more public identification with him, although it also continued stoutly to deny his involvement in politics.

The SLORC became concerned with its legitimacy, both internal and external. It became for a period more forthcoming with information, holding carefully circumscribed weekly press conferences. In January 1989, it invited a planeload of international journalists, including some known to be highly critical of the Burmese government, for a tour of Burma. However, the press was prevented from visiting bazaars and urban areas, which effectively prevented Burmese citizens from talking to them. Knowledgeable observers who read these reports easily sensed the managed nature of the tour. Other journalists were granted week-long visas for a while. Then in July 1989 reporters were barred again, even though tourist visas had been extended from one to two weeks for those in groups. Also in July international telephone lines and telexes were cut as tension mounted in Rangoon on the anniversaries associated with the abortive 1988 revolution. The regime later moderated its press policy by allowing an American television network (CNN) to visit and report on Burma in late October 1989.

The state sought to encourage the return of students from the Thai border, even offering rewards for information on them. It made arrangements with the Thai military, specifically with General Chavalit Yongchaiyut, the supreme commander, to fly army planes into Tak in Thailand to bring back students, who were then welcomed at reception centers with great public fanfare. Some three hundred were said to have returned by air.

Externally, Burma had received an extremely bad press. It was condemned by most Western governments and Amnesty International for human rights abuses, and virtually all foreign aid was cut off. Most important in economic terms was lack of recognition of the new government by Japan and its halt in assistance. With Japanese, West German, British, American, World Bank, and Asian Development Bank support in abeyance, Burma was in economic and diplomatic trouble. Only Japan withheld diplomatic recognition; the other entities expressed concern about human rights in Burma, but the degree of their protests significantly differed. The West German government, for example, wanted Burma to begin to negotiate an end to minority insurrections, while the Asian Development Bank seemed interested in resuming lending.

Finally, on February 17, 1989, Japan recognized the new government. It acted under pressure from its extensive business community, which was losing money under contracts, and because it did not want the Burmese to have to sit with the Palestine Liberation Organization and other unrecognized groups at Emperor Hirohito's funeral on February 25. Japan promised to negotiate the resumption of some current aid projects (6 grant projects worth US$75 million and 19 loan projects worth a total of US$1.5 billion), but not all were to begin again (most prominently, the extension of the Rangoon airport), and new assistance would have to await the scheduled elections.

The government tried to use its foreign legitimacy to win internal legitimacy. The visits of foreign dignitaries were played up in the local press in an attempt to demonstrate to the Burmese that the new government was well received abroad—in spite of adverse international radio broadcasts that the government could not jam.

Dealing with the Economy

The postcoup government took some beginning steps toward longer-term economic change while devoting most of its energies to short-term fundraising. On November 30, 1988, Burma promulgated its most liberal foreign investment law since independence. Although this law also encouraged public and private foreign investment in public, cooperative, and private sectors, it was clearly a longer-term program, for the uncertainties of martial law and the transition to civilian rule seemed to militate against any major productive ventures. The law was formulated in an economically and politically insecure atmosphere. When asked why foreign firms should invest now, instead of awaiting a new government that might send different economic signals, some in government answered that the liberalization was now irreversible. How many firms will eventually believe that is an unanswered question, but in the first three months of 1989, 21 limited companies and 31 new firms were registered. How many were local subsidiaries of foreign firms is unknown.

On April 1, 1989, the state announced a new set of regulations specifying those industries and fields in which the government would retain control (although joint ventures were to be allowed). These included oil and natural gas; teak extraction and sales; gems; fish and shrimp farming on government sites; post and telegraph; air and rail transportation; insurance; banking; electricity; mining and mineral exports; and armaments. The scope of these regulations is very much in line with that established by the BSPP Congress of July 23, 1988, which is said to have been determined by Ne Win.

On May 30, 1989, the Foreign Investment Commission (established on May 3) widened this scope. It publicized that investments could now be made in a broad range of fields of primary and manufactured products and could include the production, breeding, processing, marketing, and manufacturing of the newly permitted items. However, only ten foreign businesses had contacted that office by June 20.

Efforts were made to improve trade as well. Joint Venture Corporation (No. 1) was formed on April 26, 1989. It was capitalized at K50 million with ten members, seven from the government and three from internal trade organizations. Plans were to sell 50,000 shares in the corporation. However, on June 13 the *Asian Wall Street Journal* reported that this group had not yet done any business. There were six internal joint ventures by the fall, and at least an additional four involving foreign companies including those with Malaysian and Singapore firms, the latter involved in supplying armaments as well as other goods. In January 1990 the government announced that 270 contracts had been signed with foreign companies, including 9 agreements for onshore oil exploration and production.

Of more critical, immediate importance to the government were short-term measures to provide foreign exchange, local currency, and those consumer goods that the state had hoped to supply from its public enterprises, but whose production had ground to a virtual halt.

In January 1989 the military government entered into an agreement with Thailand for quick extraction of teak from designated areas along the Thai border and for fishing rights in the Tenasserim region. These projects provided the Burmese with an immediate total of US$51 million in foreign exchange—but were greeted with great concern outside of Burmese government circles. Thailand had just banned all logging because of the resultant flooding, mudslides, and loss of life near the Burma border; now Thai and Burmese critics charged both governments with exploiting Burma and perpetrating the same type of environmental rape there. General Chavalit's family was even said to have extensive interests in the agreement. Many Burmese also believed that the Thai would denude the Burmese coast of all marketable fish, because the Burmese had the capacity neither to compete technologically nor to monitor Thai adherence to the agreements on net size, number of boats, and fishing distance offshore.

Burma's government was also planning to approve a series of annual trading joint ventures with foreign firms. Under this arrangement, if such firms were to export from Burma, a certain percentage of the foreign exchange earned (higher for nontraditional exports, lower for primary product exports, such as rice, pulses, and so forth) would be allocated to these firms for imports, thus helping to bridge the gap in the availability of consumer goods. The government was also promoting a venture with Thai and other funding that would bring in US$35 million for shrimp farming. A wide range of other projects was rumored to be in the works. In late July 1989 South Korea opened a department store in Rangoon (with Burma's first escalator), in which 20 percent of the goods would be priced in kyat, the rest in foreign exchange. Burmese who had legitimate access to foreign exchange could now have foreign currency accounts.

China was not to be left out; rather, it was Burma's leading trade partner. China dominated the smuggling trade, with Burma's black market a major Chinese domain. It is only slightly hyperbolic to state that northern Burma had become a virtual Chinese economic colony, and in fact, Chinese influence was everywhere.

On August 5, 1988, Burma announced that trade with China would be regularized on October 1 of that year. Burmese citizens could now legally export virtually any product to China except rice and goods under government monopolies. Imported goods would be charged a duty, to vary by commodity. Forty percent of the value of the imported goods had to be in products that the Burmese authorities wanted and that were in short supply: in early 1989 these were toothpaste, soap, milk powder, kitchenware, and hand tillers with small trailers. This provision was dropped late in 1989. Traders were to be paid in kyat at the "prevailing" exchange rate at Shweli or Wanting, in effect a partial devaluation of the currency without explicit recognition. All of these items were supposed to be made in Burma, but the state sector had obviously failed the Burmese consumer in supplying needed goods. Observers said that only about one-third of the trade could be supervised by the Burmese and that there was collusion between traders and customs officials in undervaluing imports, thus lowering duties. Yet the government maintained that it earned K20 million per month in duties, and in December 1988 it estimated the annual volume of this trade to be US$300 million. Observers said that this represented only a small fraction of the real trade, and that the volume was closer to US$1.5 billion annually.

The official list of Burmese exports to China covered virtually all primary products produced in Burma, and the Frontier Export Division of the Yunnan People's Export Corporation noted some two thousand types of items exported to Burma. The prices of Chinese goods were low and the quality high. Chinese beer in Mandalay was cheaper (and better) than Mandalay beer. Chinese cigarettes, virtually all household goods, and even textiles were less expensive than Burmese products. A Chinese rice cooker was one-third the price of a Burmese one. Burmese school uniforms were made from Chinese cloth dyed in Burma. The Chinese swamping of the Burmese market caused major reassessments of the position of Burma's other neighbors.

Smuggling continued on these and other borders, such as those with Thailand, Bangladesh, and India. In 1988, conservative estimates indicate that perhaps 250,000 tons of rice were smuggled out. One observer indicated that 20 percent of the Arakan paddy production had gone to Bangladesh, where rice fetched over double the Burmese market prices. During Burmese fiscal year 1988–89 (ending March 31, 1989), Burma's rice exports were targeted at 80,000 tons (one-tenth of 1983–84), and during the first quarter of 1989 exports totaled 35,000 tons at a value of US$5.93 million. The second quarter rates probably rose, so estimates place exports at 110,000 to 120,000 tons.

To ease the burden of the urban people, on April 1, 1989, the Burmese government announced the first major rise in the pay scales of civil servants since the early 1950s. The minimum wage, which had been raised from K6 to K8.50 per day in August 1988 (in the middle of the demonstrations: casual laborers, numbering in the tens of thousands, were often the first to riot), was now to be K15 (less than US$2.50 at the legal rate of exchange). Although higher officials received only a 20 percent increase, lower-level staff salaries went up by 200 to 400 percent. The press was filled with stories of the military's warm-hearted concern for the people, but these salary increases, while obviously welcome, were a far cry from wages that would allow any civil servant at any level to live within the official salary. Civil servants were still forced to hold several jobs or to engage in extralegal activities. And in the summer of 1988 there were rumors that shortages of funds were preventing at least some government organizations from meeting even these inadequate pay scales. The predictable result of these increases, however justified, was rapid inflation, which some say was running between 50 and 90 percent, but which of course was underestimated in official statistics.

To avoid the crisis of 1988, when there was virtually no rice to export, the government had in effect reverted to an earlier system of forced sales of paddy to the state. In 1989 it required farmers to sell paddy to the state at K2,000 per 100 baskets of 46 pounds each (the price before liberalization was K900), which was two to three times below the market price and five times below the price in Bangladesh. The government's target for purchases was 114.9 mil-

41

lion baskets of paddy, which would allow it to export some 200,000 tons of rice and keep the remainder to provide a steady flow to the army, civil servants, and urban and rice-deficit areas. The state had learned that the unavailability or high price of rice was a sure cause of rebellion. The forced sales to the government seemed to vary by region, possibly at the discretion of each local military commander, at a rate of one-third to one-half of all production per acre. In the face of peasant complaints about the high rate of implicit taxation, the government press blamed the high prices on "rumors and politically motivated scaremongering."

The government has attempted to pay for these increased rice purchases and salaries by raising its rates for electricity, telephone use, automobile registration, and so on. Nevertheless, it seems likely that the government will have to resort to printing money to maintain its short-term stability. If so, inflation will almost certainly increase further. The martial law government may be able to suppress inflation through intimidation for a short period, but not in the longer term.

Preoccupied with short-term needs and leaving structural economic reform to the future elected government, the military regime did little planning of its own. On July 3, 1989, however, the minister of planning and finance announced: "Another goal is to change the planning process. We will accept foreign loans and assistance in economic matters when they are necessary. We shall be independent in economic matters and will not rely on foreign countries." Aung San had said the same thing more than two generations earlier. In fact, Burma will have to rely on foreign trade or aid to develop, even to survive.

In lieu of effective economic planning, the government set economic targets for the 1989–90 fiscal year. These included exports of K3.6 billion (about US$500 million at the legal rate of exchange), of which K1.3 billion was to come from the private sector. These exports goals included 791,000 metric tons of rice, 120,000 cubic feet of teak, 200,000 cubic feet of other hardwoods, and 52,000 metric tons of beans and pulses. Some of these targets seem unrealistic. Exports in the first quarter of 1989 were only K349 million, 21 percent below the same period in 1988.

Somewhat optimistically, Burmese authorities have predicted a 3 percent growth rate for 1989–90, predicated on investment of US$1.18 billion, of which only US$697.7 million is to be from the state sector. The debt service is to drop to 44.36 percent, and the gross domestic product is slated to be US$7.856 billion (at 1985–86 constant prices). The government did admit a deficit of US$286 million the previous year, and predicted one of US$628 million for 1989–90. Predictions regarding Burmese economics have proven whimsical at best, however, and whether the military can overcome the economic state of *samadhi* (suspended animation) by these moves remains to be seen. Even the military admitted that the GDP had dropped by 1.1 percent in 1986–87 and 4.2 percent in 1987–88.

On the political front, the state in 1989 was encouraging the reorganization of its new National Unity Party (NUP), effectively headed by former foreign minister Chit Hlaing, but chaired by Tha Kyaw. The NUP is perhaps one-fourth the size of the former BSPP, but it maintains an extensive network of local organizations that might prove invaluable in the future. It seems to have liberal funds for organizational work, but opposition leaders have raised questions about whether legally, as a "nongovernmental" entity, it could inherit the BSPP assets, which of course were state-funded.

The Opposition

As the state was organizing to meet the new conditions of Burmese politics, so were opposition groups. Shortly after the coup, based on the government's commitment to a multiparty system, opposition parties began to be formed, or in some cases re-formed. They were of two basic types: those within the areas controlled by the state and those on the periphery, in rebellion.

By the time the registration of political parties was closed on February 28, 1989, 233 separate parties had registered (some were later deregistered, and by December 1989 there were 207), listing their leadership and address and stating their platform and goals. Under a martial law system that still holds it illegal for more than four persons to gather together, legal political parties provide opposition groups with a protective umbrella under which to have political debates. During the early period of registration, the government also gave each party a telephone and a ration of gasoline, both of which were in short supply.

For the most part, the newly formed parties represent local interests. More than four dozen have ethnic appellations and a number of others have regional titles. Some are concerned with youth. Despite these narrow titles or focuses, most parties have broad political and economic goals, though they are rarely specified beyond the need for allowing private-sector activities within a democratic context and employment for all within Burma. They are a clear expression of the need for locally responsive government, perhaps even more than for ethnic representation.

From the government perspective, the military might argue that the very number of such parties indicates that conditions are not yet ripe for a return to civilian government; the proliferation of parties can be construed as showing that the opposition is not yet responsible and the people not yet schooled to deal with democracy.

After final registration ended and the draft election law was circulated, the process of political coalescence around various political personalities began, and at this writing still continues. Indeed, there does not seem to be a major personality in contemporary Burmese life (outside of those in rebellion) who is not publicly affiliated with some political party. Some, like Thakin Soe, the Red Flag Communist turned capitalist, had their own small entourages. (Thakin Soe died in 1989.) Other local leaders also had modest followings. Ideology seemed to play little role in this process; rather the personal pull of key leaders was most important. Alliances have been formed and broken. Analysts expect that perhaps ten groupings will eventually be formed, but by December 1989 only three critical groups had emerged.

One major group is that of Aung San Suu Kyi and Tin Oo, with whom some ninety smaller groups have affiliated. The other two main groups are led by Nu and Aung Gyi. Each has its own claim to legitimacy and its own appeal.

Nu, who now leads the League for Democracy and Peace, was Burma's last democratically elected prime minister and still describes himself as the legal prime minister, to whom the army should turn over interim power while an election is held. His key cohorts are the older generation of politicians from the 1950s. Born in 1907, Nu was a pivotal member of the student movement in the 1930s, but acquired his international fame when he took over the leadership of the AFPFL from the assassinated Aung San. His following is devoted, and his appeal is to a strong, older Buddhist element, who regarded him as having almost saintly qualities. His following among the younger Burmese seems limited.

Brigadier Aung Gyi, retired, born in 1918, is seven years younger than Ne Win. He is regarded as a liberal socialist, and many say he fully expected to take over from Ne Win on at least two occasions after the 1962 coup. Most recently, he was credited with placating the mob before the Ministry of Defense just before the latest coup, when it was rumored he was to form an interim government. (Some vilified him for this action.) He was publicly critical of the government during the spring of 1988 through a series of quasi-

44

public letters he wrote to Ne Win, in which he carefully avoided personal criticism of Ne Win but attacked the sycophants around him. (Some even say Ne Win encouraged these letters and their publicity.)

Aung Gyi has been jailed on several occasions. Originally the leader of the Aung San Suu Kyi–Tin Oo group, he was expelled in early December 1988 when he claimed that Suu Kyi was being influenced by communist advisers, a charge that General Khin Nyunt has subsequently reiterated on many occasions. Aung Gyi then founded the rival Union Nationals Democratic Party. He is staunchly anticommunist. Aung Gyi's is the only organization that has explicitly discussed negotiating an end to the ethnic insurrections before the elections and that seems to favor a more liberal sharing of the economic pie with the ethnic minorities. He has lost ground, however, at least among youth, because they feel he let down the revolution by counseling the people to trust the army.

The National League for Democracy is led by Aung San Suu Kyi (general secretary) and Tin Oo (chairman). Suu Kyi, the only daughter of Aung San (she has a brother who lives in San Diego), has spent most of her life abroad. Married to an Englishman—an Oxford academician specializing in Tibet and Central Asia—she herself has academic interests. She returned to Burma before the summer of 1988 to be with her dying mother, and apparently with the vaguely defined idea of making a political contribution to a future Burma. Her timely presence, the blossoming of her capacity to deal with crowds, and the aura she created produced a large following.

Suu Kyi was joined by the very popular retired general Tin Oo, who had been jailed by Ne Win for knowledge of (but not involvement in) an attempted coup by younger officers in 1976. He added an important degree of credibility to this group.

Aung San Suu Kyi has drawn large crowds whenever she has campaigned in rural or provincial areas. Sometimes, as in the Irrawaddy Delta, she has been harassed by the local military; on whose initiative remains in question. Suu Kyi is said to have 3 million supporters, the most of any opposition figure. Under house arrest since July 1989, she has been disqualified from participating in the May 1990 elections. Tin Oo was sentenced to three years' hard labor in December 1989, and many NLD supporters have also been jailed.

The student groups have a number of small parties, but they are less important than the general role of the students themselves and their leaders. Many of the students are underground, organized into small, secret cells to prevent betrayal to the state. The military has recognized the capacity of the students to organize antigovernment activities, from major rallies to small "hit-and-run" demonstrations. With less to lose, and less hope in their personal futures for jobs and mobility, the students represent a critical force with which any present or future government will have to deal. This confrontation has never stopped: on the first anniversary of the March riots of 1988 and in the two-week period following, until Armed Forces Day, some small demonstrations were conducted, including a number led by student groups. The government moved to arrest many student leaders including the best known, Min Ko Naing.

Opposition along the Borders
On the periphery, astride the China border, the Burma Communist Party (BCP) was the major insurgent force intent upon overthrowing the Rangoon government. The BCP had advocated the formation of an interim government and was bitterly opposed to the 1988 coup. The BCP played no role in the political events of 1988, for it sought only to protect its share of the border trade with China and its opium smuggling operations, on which it has in large part relied since the Chinese withdrew support almost a decade ago.

In an event that may have been unique among world communist parties at that time, the Burma Communist Party collapsed through internal revolution. The Wa peoples made up the bulk of BCP forces, since the BCP operated largely in Wa territory. On the evening of April 16, 1989, they revolted against the BCP leadership and forced many leaders over the border into China. There were claims that the cause of this collapse was an inappropriate strategy: the BCP leadership favored a Maoist rural revolution, but the antigovernment ferment in 1988 was in urban areas. However, factional and ethnic issues must have also played a role.

Strategic concerns aside, the communist movement in Burma had clearly been losing strength for many years. The areas it once depended on are now controlled by tribal leaders, who also engage in opium trading and are perhaps more willing than the BCP was to join with other rebels. This change may affect the military balance in the region, allowing the Burmese government to move troops away from this area, directing its forces against the Kachin or other minority rebels instead. The destruction of the BCP also means that there are now no organized forces in Burma overtly bent on the overthrow of the Rangoon government (although students along the Thai border have such a goal). Even though the BCP has collapsed, the SLORC has used the threat of "BCP methods" as one reason for its repressive actions, and as late as August 1989 General Khin Nyunt in a major speech linked the communists to a generalized incipient revolution in 1988, and more specifically to the National League for Democracy and Aung San Suu Kyi.

More important than the BCP is the newly formed Democratic Alliance for Burma, which is composed of 23 different groups outside of the legal control of the state. Headed by Bo Mya, of the Karen, its vice president is the Kachin leader, Brang Sang. Mon and Burman leaders also are involved. The Democratic Alliance has been joined by a militant Burman Buddhist organization, the *Yahan Pyo Aphwe* (Young Monks' Association), and by some of the Burmese students who fled to the border. This group has also called for an interim government and is prepared to negotiate some role for minority regions into a federal structure for Burma.

Significantly, in its first recognition of the need to deal with the minority regions by some means other than military, the SLORC founded the Work Committee for the Development of the Border Region and the Indigenous Nationals in May 1989. It also plans to develop programs for those regions, based in Kunlong for the Wa area and in Keng Tung for the eastern Shan state. However, no programs have yet been announced, and much of the region is not even under central government control.

Extensive military campaigns were initiated against the various insurgents, especially the Karen and the Mon. Indications in November 1989 were that a campaign might soon begin against the 10,000-man Kachin Independence Army as well.

1989 and Beyond

In regimes where violence has been an instrument of repression, anniversaries assume a particular salience. The summer of 1989 was replete with anniversaries of the events of 1988 and earlier: the July 7, 1962, destruction of the Rangoon University student union; the July 19 Martyrs' Day, marking the 1947 assassination of Aung San and his cabinet; and so on for each stage in the protest movement, culminating in the first anniversary of the coup on September 18, 1989.

In defiance of martial law, the National League for Democracy held rallies in Rangoon which drew crowds in the thousands, building up pressure on the government. Suu Kyi was arrested on June 21, then quickly released; one person was killed in the demonstrations. There were charges that the government had already

47

arrested many that spring; the number was not known but Suu Kyi claimed that about 1,000 dissidents had been jailed since March 1.

As tension built, General Saw Maung gave a major speech on July 5, warning the opposition against such actions and promising stern reprisals. Protest gatherings, he declared, would only be allowed three months before the 1990 elections, at which time the press would also be freed from restrictions. Suu Kyi appeared to give in. As Martyrs' Day approached, she called off the planned demonstrations, for the military presence was building up in Rangoon and the army was reinforcing its troops with an additional 10 percent of its total forces.

Nevertheless, on July 20 the army placed Aung San Suu Kyi and General Tin Oo under house arrest for at least a year (Tin Oo was later jailed). In late October 1989 the government announced that those under arrest could not be nominated for office. Thus, Suu Kyi and Tin Oo will be effectively prevented from participating directly in the elections (and in January 1990 Suu Kyi was explicitly barred from doing so). Candidates for election must have registered six months before the election to qualify. In addition, they cannot be associated with any illegal group (such as those involved in the insurgencies) or have received foreign support; there are other requirements, including "full" citizenship. At the time of Suu Kyi's arrest the government specified that her party would not be affected, but few believed that this move was not in fact aimed at destruction of the National League for Democracy, the most effective opposition group; many members of that group were jailed under various pretexts. How the population will react to this move should the elections take place as scheduled and should the National League for Democracy remain emasculated is an important question.

Other events have called into question the sincerity of the military's claim to be loosening control over the society. For example, the government announced that the elections scheduled for May 1990 (and for which the information required for registration is extensive) would not be for a new government, but rather for a convention charged with writing a new constitution. This implies that the military will retain ultimate authority or remain in power even after May 27, 1990. If so, direct military government would continue through the writing of a new constitution and the holding of a referendum (now normal practice) on it; that is, the military might remain in direct control in some manner until 1992. Whether directly or indirectly, the influence of the military on a new constitution and the distribution of power is likely to be profound.

IV. The Underlying Crisis in the Political Economy

The antecedents of the present crisis are sometimes obscure, always complex. They may be as basic as the slow but perceptible changes during the last few decades in the social system and in the role of elites or as palpable as the economic power of foreign groups over the Burmese economy. The paucity of data, the absence of research, and the lack of a Burmese climate encouraging self-inquiry mean that any conclusions must be highly tentative. Yet these issues need to be explored if contemporary Burma and its choices are to be understood.

Changes in Burmese Social Structure

Burmese social structure is in the process of undergoing important changes that will affect the future of the state and the distribution of its assets. Although highly diverse ethnic, linguistic, and social systems coexist within the minority one-third of Burma's population, this section will deal with the Burman two-thirds of the population; that is, with those who speak Burmese as their native language, are almost universally Buddhist, and wear their own distinctive dress. Minorities are not necessarily excluded from this dominant culture, but because they exist within an overwhelmingly Burman culture, they are influenced by Burman perceptions of history, culture, and the external world.

Burmans generally inhabit the central plains and the Irrawaddy Delta of Burma, with a heartland in the Mandalay region. They are a sedentary, rice-growing, and rice-consuming population. Burma, more specifically the Burman area of Burma, is unique among those Asian states that were colonized by Europeans: it is the only area where the ruling precolonial elites disappeared during the colonial period and did not reappear in some positions of authority after independence. There did not reemerge in Burma the equivalent of a mandarin or literati class based on wealth, bureaucratic power, and social esteem, as happened with the *yangban* (Confucian gentry) in South Korea, or with such royal elites as the sultan of Jogjakarta, Indonesia, the maharajahs of India, and others. The vast preindependence estates common in the Philippines did not exist in Burma, so there was no major oligarchical elite. Rather, when the king and royal family were exiled from Burma to India at the end of the Third Anglo-Burmese War in 1886, the elite class virtually collapsed. Most senior appointments had been dependent on the royal personage, and thus the end of the monarchy meant the end of the traditional ruling class among Burmans. This was in marked distinction to the hereditary ruling systems in some of the Burmese minority groups, such as the Shan and Kayah, who were able to retain until 1959 their sophisticated hereditary and hierarchical ruling structure headed by the *sawbwas*, who were a kind of maharajah. These and other minority groups were ruled separately from the Burmans by the British.

Colonial elites among the Burmans did develop as products of service to the British Crown; they were normally required to have a knowledge of English and often, at the highest level, a British education. These colonial elites were significant in the bureaucratic milieu (within the Burma Civil Service, for example), but after independence they were subordinate to the Burmese politicians, who arose from a broad social spectrum of the population and who gained fame from the nationalist movement that the civil servants tended to avoid.

At the time of independence, Burma enjoyed a highly mobile social system. There were few differences in attitude between the urban power elite and the villagers, as existed in so many other societies. It was quite common to see sons and daughters of the rural poor enrolled at the Universities of Rangoon or Mandalay. Leadership often came from those with peasant or petit-bourgeois backgrounds.

There were four essential avenues to social mobility in civilian Burma: education, the *sangha* (monkhood), the political process, and the military. Each was important and produced its own illustrious figures.

Female participation in education at all levels was high, and literacy was more common than in any other country in the region. Since traditional schools were monastic, there was a close emotional correlation between Buddhist piety and literacy. There was equal access to education through state and, in more remote villages, monastic schools. Education was free through the university level, and both sons and daughters of a wide range of the population, including minority groups, attended Burma's two universities. Those sent abroad by the government as state scholars were bright and motivated. There was virtually no "brain drain" from Burma before 1962; scholars returned from abroad to take up responsible positions at extremely low salaries, and there seemed to be a gen-

50

eral (though undocumented) satisfaction with the Burmese lifestyle among the educated.

The *sangha* was only open to males, but for them it was a personally and socially rewarding experience that also served as an important avenue of mobility. Virtually all Buddhist males entered the *sangha* for at least a short period, and they could leave at any time without stigma. Poor boys could receive free monastic education through primary school, and then continue through university within the Buddhist educational system. One who left the *sangha* did so with added prestige and status. In 1989 the government announced that there were about 300,000 in the *sangha*, of whom 120,000 were monks and 180,000 were novices or junior members. In addition, 20,000 nuns composed a less prestigious religious category.

With independence and the blossoming of the political process came the formation of political mass organizations that allowed the motivated, the poor, and the marginally educated to assume positions of local and even national importance. Leadership in such groups as the All-Burma Peasants' Organization and workers' associations, as well as in political parties, was a means of climbing to national attention, and a number of early leaders in Burma did precisely that.

Equally important was the military, which was designed to recruit to officer status those bright men who were also highly motivated. The military was perceived to be a desirable career, and although a universal draft law was passed in 1959 under the military caretaker government, it was never implemented, since volunteers more than made up the quota. A man might rise by promotion from the ranks; through the Officer Training School (often with some previous higher education); or by being selected to attend the Burma Military Academy at Maymyo, the Burmese West Point. Graduates of the Academy received University of Rangoon degrees.

Although the Burmese government was highly centrist, there was still room for local leadership. Politicians in both Burma Proper and the minority states were generally responsive to local needs through the loose party process. An Arakanese political party was especially effective.

Then, after the coup of 1962, Burma's social system became highly integrated and centrally controlled. The mass political organizations were brought under the control of the military, first directly and then through the BSPP. No organization was allowed to exist without the state imprimatur.

51

In spite of its protests, the *sangha* was finally registered in 1980 after a long battle over attempted state control. Monks were ordered to carry identity cards that indicated by whom they had been ordained. This was designed to rid the organizations of "bogus" or "subversive" monks—those who slipped in and out at will, using the *sangha* to obtain immunity from state persecution or prosecution.

Education expanded after 1962, when all private (mostly missionary-founded) schools were nationalized. There was a growth of state schools at all levels, with a determined effort by the government to increase higher education. This was done through expanded enrollment and the reorganization of existing schools, and through correspondence courses by which workers could earn university degrees. After the student demonstrations in 1974, Ne Win decided to form vocational community colleges in each division or state. His ostensible purpose was to provide training to improve economic development at the local level, but his actual agenda was to keep students out of Rangoon and Mandalay, where their actions were a greater threat to government.

In fact, the regional college system accomplished neither objective. The vocational training program was poorly integrated into the job market and poorly executed as well. Students continued to proliferate in the main urban centers, while regional businesses could not benefit from the newly trained regional graduates, since the private sector was not encouraged in other ways. Much academic time was devoted to political indoctrination, further lowering standards already reduced by fear of teaching politically inappropriate subjects, such as capitalistic economy, and by outmoded teaching materials. All research was considered classified until released by the government.

After the government had expanded higher education, it began to impose fees, making access for the poor more difficult. Further, it denied admittance to noncitizens, mostly those of Indian and Chinese parentage. And as education expanded, quality fell. Salaries for teachers were frozen while the cost of living rose, and schools were closed for long periods because of the threat of student demonstrations. Teachers went in search of additional income, while students turned to private education to supplement the failing public system. Thus arose the ubiquitous tutoring schools to help students pass examinations, for which fees (from K50 to K1000 per month) varied according to the exclusiveness and level of the instruction. Although statistics show that state expenditures in education between 1965 and 1979 rose almost threefold in current kyat, in fact during that period expenditures in constant currency fell by some 15 percent, and by far more on a per capita basis. Thus although official statistics suggested that education was expanding and offering increased mobility, in fact the state was spending less on education and restricting entry into the elite system.

The military continued to be the primary avenue to mobility and economic success. A Soviet-style system of state stores was established, access to which was based on military rank. Although it was originally intended to provide necessities nowhere else available, it soon became a premier means by which elites could gain access to valuable commodities in short supply and resell them on the black market, thus supplementing their still-meager incomes. However, only 500 officers were produced every year: 200 from the Defense Services Academy, 200 from the Officers Training School, and 100 promoted from the ranks. The military in turn determined who could enter this upper stratum of society. Since the military controlled the party and the bureaucracy, and since examinations for entry into the civil service were based not on technical competence but on political factors, the army was virtually in complete control of the social system. Present and former military staffed key posts in most ministries and corporations. They were then able to provide entry for their children to colleges, the civil service, and other positions of power. In contrast to South Korea, which after the military coup of 1961 opened up a variety of avenues for social mobility, Burma in 1962 began to close them off, keeping only the military road open. The military in Burma differed from that in the Philippines as well. Whereas the latter has been described as protecting elite interests, in Burma the military had become the elite.

When Burma began to open to the rest of the world in the mid-1970s, opportunities for foreign travel and study were largely limited to the elite's children, reinforcing their high status. Such travel also gave opportunities legally to bring in commodities that could earn the traveler profits of up to K100,000 (US$15,000) on a single trip. A student who stayed abroad for an extended period could bring back a pickup truck and earn enough from that transaction alone to live on for years. Thus the military was able to perpetuate its privileged position.

In spite of the military's control and the unitary nature of the state, the BSPP was expanding to become a mass party by 1971. At the same time, significant local political debate was developing. This was not, however, reflected in the press nor in the highly orchestrated *Pyithu Hluttaw* proceedings, which were meticulously

53

scripted. Membership in that body was not based on leadership from local regions, but rather given to stalwart party or military personnel who were assigned districts (perhaps on a British parliamentary model) from which to run. Under the single-party system, they never lost. The result was that intellectual diversity gradually disappeared at the local level, and political apathy set in. The system became even more stratified, less mobile, and more highly centralized. One former BSPP Central Executive Committee member remarked in 1988: "After 26 years, we had become corrupt, stratified, and generally stupid."

Urbanization and Employment

According to government statistics, Burma's population is growing at an annual rate of 2.0 percent. Some observers believe the rate may be significantly higher due to a pronatalist policy, reportedly imposed by Ne Win personally out of fear of the massive number of peoples on Burma's borders, and perhaps fear of Burma's minorities as well. Although official figures indicate that Burma now only farms about one-half of its arable land, and thus has unusually low population pressures on its rural areas, much of this land is in insecure areas or in minority regions that are regarded as indefensible or inhospitable to the majority Burman population. In addition, stringent government policies have made rural employment unattractive; there have been few incentives for peasants. Until the fall of 1987, the fixed prices of all major crops were low. Under the military, not only does the state own all the land (which has been true of all governments since independence), but more important, land cannot be deeded to heirs without local party approval. Notices have occasionally appeared in the press indicating that if farmers do not adhere to state regulations on cropping or sales, their land, residually owned by the state, could be confiscated. There are few private incentives for capital improvements in rural Burma; nor can the government afford them. Although the state has wanted to expand its direct rural holdings through state farms and through the parastatal cooperative movement, these goals have never been achieved.

The result has been a rise in the urban population, in large part through migration, although infant mortality in urban areas is likely to be much lower than the national average. Although the data may be incomplete, in 1983 one-third of the Burmese population was listed as urban (8.5 million urban dwellers and 25.7 million rural). Rangoon, the primary city, had a population of more than three million (from only 737,000 in 1953) and Mandalay of more than half a million. At the time of the 1962 coup, each was only about one-fifth that size.

While the urban population was expanding, employment opportunities were essentially static. The state had recognized this problem as early as 1971, when the party officially published its first major critique of the economic system, *The Long-Term and Short-Term Economic Policies of the Burma Socialist Programme Party*. In this document, the BSPP noted that public-sector employment was essentially fixed, and that since the private sector was not being encouraged, there were few jobs available. The public sector was already too large. In 1965 it was 456,000, and in 1971, 776,000 (including 513,000 in state corporations), but by 1976 it was 1,009,000 (all of these figures exclude the military). Yet unemployment figures, based on an essentially irrelevant labor exchange, continued to be low and misleading. Unofficially, urban unemployment was calculated at 9.4 percent in 1973; normally the unemployment rate among youth would be two to three times as high. Even as early as 1970, unemployed university graduates were said to total 18,000.

For the next 17 years the government did virtually nothing to alleviate a problem that proved to be cancerous. By 1988, less than 20 percent of the engineering graduates from the Rangoon Institute of Technology could find positions in their fields. The state graduated some six hundred doctors each year (half of them women), but few could be employed. College graduates were driving pedicabs. The extended family system did provide a type of economic safety net, but the monstrous unemployment remained both politically dangerous and a disastrous waste of talent.

After the riots of 1974, which had been led by students and youth, the government was forced to recognize the problem. It quietly began to allow citizens to leave Burma, some to find employment as merchant sailors (a highly lucrative profession because it enabled one to import scarce commodities), but more to work abroad in any capacity. Previously, ever since the 1962 coup, emigration had been illegal. Those who left generally walked into Thailand, often at considerable danger. This exodus had now become accepted, a tragic result of the military control system that provided few economic incentives and virtually no political or intellectual freedom. Since the 1988 coup, the "drain" has become a virtual flood, as the government rids itself of unemployed, dissident intellectuals.

Since it was the educated who left Burma, much of the trained talent disappeared. Although figures are lacking, perhaps 1 percent of the total population of Burma is now abroad: more than 100,000 in North America, 35,000 in Australia, 35,000 in Europe, and the remainder in Southeast Asia, mostly Thailand. The drive to leave is strong. In March 1989 when the United States held a worldwide lottery for immigration visas, more than 50 sellers of applications were counted within a few blocks in the streets of downtown Rangoon in a single day. Many expatriates remit taxes to Burma in foreign exchange, which makes their exodus economically as well as politically welcome in the short term, but a serious depletion over the long run.

The Economic Issues

Burma effectively entered the world market under British direction in the 19th century, having been first subjected to the unfamiliar rigors of a monetized economy. At that time, Burmans had little control over the economic forces that directly affected their lives. Major internal and external trade, credit, and production were essentially in foreign hands. Burmans were virtually excluded from their own military (in 1940 only about 13 percent of the Burmese military was Burman). The civil service and the professions were dominated by immigrants from India, as were many menial urban jobs. Burma was governed from India until 1937, and Burma's colonial masters encouraged both temporary and permanent Indian immigration.

When the global depression of the 1930s struck Burma, it was the Burmans who were most directly hurt, especially those in the rich rice-growing areas of the south. Divorced from the modern sector of the economy, and with about four-fifths of their rice land in foreign hands or mortgaged, mainly to Indians, they viewed the world economy as both alien and exploitative. With the Indian and Chinese communities in control of the local economy, Burmans were essentially relegated to petty bazaar trading. Equating capitalism with imperialism, virtually all the leaders of the independence movement in the 1930s became socialists; socialism was seen as the means by which the Burmans could regain control over their economic lives.

The British had intentionally insulated Burma from fashionable foreign intellectual trends, such as Fabian socialism. But by the 1930s Burmese students in England had brought back these ideas.

56

The influence of the Indian nationalist movement provided further impetus to the independence struggle. The socialist concepts that entered Burma had no equivalent in the Burmese language, so the new terms were adopted from Pali, the language of Burmese Buddhism, which gave the concepts added legitimacy. Since Buddhist monks had been active in the nationalist movement since the 1920s (as the British had banned political, but not religious, organizations), nationalism, Buddhism, and socialism were united.

Everyone assumed that an independent Burma would be socialist to some degree. Until late 1988, every Burmese government since independence has reaffirmed that goal. When Nu in 1955 called for more private enterprise to invigorate an economic system he saw as both corrupt and failing, he did so within the socialist construct. When Ne Win in 1971 called for "mutually beneficial economic enterprises" with foreign private investors, he too was speaking from within socialism. Likewise, the July 23, 1988, BSPP congress that tried to restructure the economy by encouraging foreign and domestic private investment included no criticism of the socialist basis of the state.

The *dirigiste* tendencies in the Burmese body politic have always been strong and remain so. Although the term "socialism" has virtually been banned from use by the government since the 1988 coup, the state has reasserted its intention to retain control over a variety of key industries including banking, oil, teak, and gem production. It is not about to let loose the private sector, although the reins around it will be relaxed.

Burma has made recurring efforts at economic reform. At each stage, political imperatives have become paramount, driving out economic rationality, with each government modifying the economic system only on the fringes and giving up as little authority as it could. This, of course, is not unusual in any society, but in Burma the degree of political sensitivity seems higher than in many other places, and the fear of offending those in political power, since such power is so highly personalized, has been more pervasive.

To regard Burma's incentives for economic growth as limited by Buddhism is to discount Burmese economic reality. There is little doubt that, despite Buddhist detachment, Burmans appreciate the benefits of material comfort, if only because it provides the leisure for meditation and earning Buddhist merit. The alacrity with which Burman farmers in the 19th century migrated from independent Burma in the north into the British-ruled Irrawaddy Delta as soon as it was opened to rice cultivation is a classic instance of Burman responsiveness to economic opportunities.

However, the lack of many social incentives for the accumulation of wealth, the fear of harassment for being economically different, the likelihood of state intervention in the productive process, and a general attitude that trade is not itself productive have all militated against Burman participation in much of modern economic life. The relative newness of a completely monetized economy probably also negatively affected Burman participation in the modern economic sector. Those factors, in combination with the advantageous position of Chinese and Indians, who had access to credit based on clan, family, or caste affiliations, dissuaded most Burmans from competing in the marketplace.

In the recent past, a Burman with a little money was far better off either building a pagoda or going into the smuggling trade than going into business: by building a pagoda he would receive a long-term karmic return on his investment; by smuggling he would receive a short-term financial gain. Incentives for production were minimal, and there was little to buy, at least legally.

Burma's fear of foreign economic domination has persisted far beyond the reality of external conditions. This fear has become a state-sponsored ritual response: foreigners will exploit us if they have the economic opportunity, so it is better to be poor and retain our culture than to abandon our culture and morals for the sake of modernity. This attitude is widespread and virulent because it emanates from the top of Burma's hierarchy. Ethnic prejudices have become combined with economic fear, each feeding the other. It is no accident that communal rioting has often taken place at times of economic hardship. Nor is it unusual for the government to direct economic anger away from itself and onto the minorities, as it did against the Chinese in 1967 and may also have done against Muslims in July 1988.

Burma's abundant natural resources lie on its periphery, in areas either held by the insurgents or under insecure government control. These areas and their potential are denied to the state; in some cases (such as teak and gem production) they have provided some of the economic means by which the insurgents are able to maintain their decades-long rebellions. Resolving its minority issues is one means by which the state might garner the resources it needs for stronger economic performance.

Power and Politics

The possible reemergence of a multiparty political system raises the issue of the past efficacy of such a system in Burma. It also raises the question of whether either a military regime or a single-party, formerly socialist state—or in Burma's case, both simultaneously- —can make such a transition. World events suggest this may in fact be possible. In 1989, Hungary, Poland, East Germany, Czechoslovakia, Bulgaria, and Romania rapidly proceeded down liberalizing, although different, paths. Spain has moved from a military dictatorship of several decades into a democratic regime strong enough to put down a military coup (though it had a king to help in that process). Tunisia "retired" its founding president and liberalized a single-party system. The economic reforms in Eastern Europe and China have led to pressures for political reform as well, though governments often attempt to separate the need for economic liberalism from the desire for political pluralism.

Some economic liberalization has begun in Burma. And the promise of political pluralism has been made. Some of the formalities, such as diverse political parties, have been established. But the concepts of shared power and authority have yet to be fully integrated into Burmese political life. Whereas the government in Hungary sponsored a major reformist demonstration in April 1989 to try to preempt dissident groups, and in Poland an opposition Solidarity leader became prime minister in August 1989, in Burma the state has attempted to quell student and other demonstrations by dispersing them and arresting their leaders. The government has admitted to arresting 251 people between mid-March and mid-June 1989. Other observers say thousands have been arrested since March 1989. Some one hundred have been sentenced to death. Many believe that the emptying of the jails (more than 19,000 inmates were released by August 1989) was done so that they could be filled with political dissidents.

There is without question a strong outcry for a multiparty system in Burma. This demand is pervasive and has been made even by Ne Win (who may have wanted to reform the BSPP through multiparty competition). This does not necessarily mean that the Burmese want a state that would allow the freedoms that are normally associated with democracy, or even with some more circumscribed concept of political pluralism. It may rather be more reflective of the nation's total disillusionment with the BSPP, and thus with any rigid political system that tends to reward political conformity over efficiency and innovation. In fact, BSPP incompetence and overall rigidity became evident as soon as it gained control.

It can plausibly be argued that the civilian regime's freedoms of press and expression were not an outgrowth of a general belief in such principles, but rather reflected a delicate balance between competing political powers when no single center could exert the authority it would have desired. The history of modern, independent Burma is still too short to encourage generalizations, but we should ask whether its possession of the concept of an inherent value in freedom of information, association, or expression has yet been illustrated. Those who have advocated those rights have generally opposed the system in power; those in power may have only seemed to advocate those rights when their complex political alliances required restraint of their own authority.

The call for a multiparty system and democracy may be simply a vote against the BSPP; it could also be for some an institutional mechanism to seize power. The call for democracy may thus be a means to a less-than-democratic end. Yet an international trend toward more popular and representative governments is evident, and Burma may be caught up in this movement. The vigor of the press during the civilian era does offer promise for the future.

Likewise, the resurgence of economic liberalism in Burma does not necessarily imply that political liberalism must follow, as events in China in June 1989 and thereafter so horribly illustrated. In Burma, strong elements from both the right (within the army for the most part) and the left (above and underground) are currently opposed to political liberalism. The military, including some opposition leaders such as Aung Gyi, have long records of concern about communist infiltration, and they tend to view broad freedoms as allowing these leftist elements to assume more powerful roles. Nor is there much likelihood that the far left would ensure a vocal, free opposition if it had power.

As long as power in Burma continues to be seen in personal terms, and as long as power is regarded as a fixed quantity, so that sharing or delegating it diminishes one's own stature, it will be exceedingly difficult to institutionalize an effective pluralistic system in Burma.

In addition, Burma's post-1962 governments have not encouraged civic pluralism. Traditionally, few autonomous civic groups (as distinguished from professional ones) have developed among Burmans; the absence of these organizations restricted the possibility of organized social pressures from below. Exceptions are religious and ethnic minorities, such as the Muslims, perhaps because of the perceived threats to them and their need to protect their membership. However, as urbanization increases, the gradual development of other autonomous organizations can be expected.

External Relations and Xenophobia

There are valid and enduring reasons why the Burmans should feel insecure within their own state. From their perspective, they have been politically colonized and economically deprived for almost two centuries. They have seen the Indian and Chinese minorities in their society assume economic power far in excess of their populations. They have seen their indigenous minorities governed separately under colonial rule, and preference given to them in retention of their ruling elites and tribal ways, as well as in various types of employment. They have felt both colonial and contemporary foreign prejudice in favor of those minorities who adopted Christianity and seen that these groups have sometimes been in closer contact with foreigners than with their own central government.

Burmans are surrounded by neighbors that dwarf them in population. They have seen foreign incursions into their territory (the *Kuomintang*, for example) and foreign support for them (the United States in the 1950s), as well as informal sustenance given by foreign governments to rebels (the Chinese to the Burma Communist Party; the Thai to the Shan, Karen, and Nu; the Bengalis to the Arakanese rebels; the Indians to the Chin and Naga). Burmans' economic lifeline—commodity exports—is subject to buffeting by international commodity prices over which they have no control and to which very little value is added, and so they must either borrow from abroad or depend on the largess of donors.

Many Burmans feel their culture is under attack from an international, Westernizing trend that, in Burmese eyes, has already destroyed Bangkok. Ne Win was against the introduction of television into Burma because he felt it would corrupt the culture, and was only persuaded when it was agreed that television would be solely educational and without advertisements. Burmese men fear that their women will be seduced by Muslims or Westerners. The Burmese believe that their society is fragile and sensitive and must be protected from foreigners. The slogans that appear constantly in the government-controlled *Working People's Daily* exhorting the populace to preserve their culture may be interpreted as indirect expressions of anxiety.

At the same time, Burmans have enormous pride in their culture and in the fact that they have sustained it while other states have become internationalized. Burmans are comfortable with their mores and believe in their unique contribution to world civilization, to the Buddhist canon, and to the propagation of Buddhism. They proudly recognize the regional power of the Burmese state at various stages in its history. They conceive of their internal role as civilizing the ruder peoples on their frontiers and their external role as being an exemplary neutral nation.

These conflicting sentiments have produced a set of attitudes that tend to create considerable official suspicion of foreign motives, however open, honest, and delightful personal relationships between individual Burmese and foreigners may be. Foreigners are seen as intent on despoiling Burma and the Burmese. Many Burmans believe that Burma is being discriminated against in international affairs because of its neutrality. The public has been officially urged to identify Burmese citizens with foreign sympathies "and eradicate them like maggots from the country's flesh." "To like foreign foods, for example, shows that the person concerned is not quite aesthetically Myanmar," the *Working People's Daily* noted. "Entertain grave doubts about the patriotism and nationalism as well as the claims that they love the country and the people, made by those who show such alien preferences. The lackeys within the country lick the boots of the long noses and try to please them, making the prestige of the Myanmar people held in low esteem." These are representative of comments frequently heard or read.

The government, of course, uses these attitudes to foster its own plans, to explain away its own mistakes, and to redirect internal resentment against the outside. To the extent that it is able to control information and the free flow of ideas, these attitudes may gain credibility.

Those Burmese who have long been exposed to foreign influences through, for example, study abroad, are therefore required to prove their Burmese identity in some extraordinary way. The official press quoted the minister of health and education as saying that those who go abroad for study should not look down on their country, and "they ought not to think highly of foreign countries either." Yet Burma needs external knowledge to compete effectively in the world rice and other markets, to develop technological skills in mining and medicine, and to plan its economy and institutional development better, even as Burmese fear that such knowledge is somehow destabilizing of their culture and society. As the official press has written, "The first priority is the preservation of our national values, our dignity and our cultural heritage; following this we may seek material progress and development without affecting our cultural heritage. We certainly would never abandon our culture and morals for the sake of modernity."

There has been an official cultural campaign against foreigners, the Western "long noses" and the "black" Indians. Long articles have pointed out past economic injustices, the despoiling of Burmese women, the loose morals of foreigners. These influences have been contrasted to the purity of Burman ethics and life, which must be preserved. If continued, this campaign can only lead to heightened tension both internally and between the Burmese and the foreigners they hope will come to the economic rescue of Burma. If there are economic failures, the groundwork has been prepared to blame foreigners.

Each society has its own special set of dichotomies. In the Burmese case, the dichotomy between the need for and the distrust of foreign knowledge is particularly acute because Burma's economic crisis has occurred at a time when international technology (radio, television, telephones, computers, and fax machines) no longer gives Burma the luxury of isolation, and when Burma's neighbors and competitors are moving ahead rapidly in economics and in politics. Burma's choices for the future are both urgent and difficult.

V. Burma's Choices for the Future

The momentous, virtually unprecedented choices facing Burma in 1990 can be viewed as several distinct Cartesian decisions. In practice, however, these issues are unlikely to be addressed so coherently, consistently, or logically as any analytical framework might suggest.

Burma's choices can be grouped under two broad categories: center-periphery issues and external relations. Center-periphery issues are concerned with Burma's internal affairs: the constitutional distribution of power; the multiparty process; military-civilian relations and the role of class; the ethnic regions and their rebellions, including issues of narcotics production, refining, sales, and distribution; central planning and local initiative; and cultural diversity with national unity.

The second-category issues relate to Burma's external relations. They include the basic question of how Burma will respond to broad foreign influences, but also such concerns as Burmese neutralism and isolationism; participation in international commerce, trade, and investment; the international technological and informational revolution and Burma's place in such a milieu; the increasingly important relations with China, Thailand, and India and their rivalries with regard to Burma; and the role of the United States.

Center-Periphery Relations

Although Ne Win ruled by decree from 1962 until 1974, and the SLORC has done the same since the coup of 1988, one of the first acts of any new government following the elections (or any military attempt to convert to a civilian government without them, as in 1974) will be to write a new constitution. In effect, the new government will function as a kind of constitutional convention. For the military to take on that task prior to or in lieu of elections would destroy the credibility of the results.

The Constitution and the Political Process. For the constitutions of 1947 and 1974, the critical issue was the distribution of power between a strong central government (dominated by Burmans) and the periphery (the minority peoples and regions). For each constitution, intense sets of negotiations preceded the final decision. The two results were, however, antithetical.

In 1947, in preparation for independence from the British, Burma had to find a way to include its minorities. To this end, in February 1947 a meeting at Panglong in the Shan state brought together most of the major minority groups. Had no compromise been reached, Burma might have become two or more potentially hostile states, or its independence might have been substantially delayed.

The major ethnic groups attended, although the Karen were only observers, not participants. The Panglong Agreement (today celebrated on Union Day, with extensive ethnic pageantry) was the basis on which subsequent negotiations concluded that Burma was to have partly self-governing entities in important minority areas: Kachin, Shan, and Kayah states and Chin Special Division (a province). A Karen state was added later. Each entity was to have a modest amount of local autonomy and would be represented in one house of a bicameral legislature, the Chamber of Nationalities.

The Shan and Kayah states had the most sophisticated hereditary local rulers, who had actually remained in positions of reduced power under the British. In fact, the Kayah state had been a separate protectorate of the British, and its independence had been recognized by both the British and the Burmese court as early as 1875. To placate the Shan and Kayah states, Burma gave them the right to secede from the new Union of Burma after a plebiscite that could be held after ten years. The Kachin state was denied that right because it contained a substantial number of Burmans. In fact, no future Burmese government could have allowed any secession to take place, for political reasons. The resulting structure was a mix unknown elsewhere, with no precedent in Burmese history either. It worked to neither side's satisfaction, but no other approach seemed feasible at that time.

In 1968 Ne Win called together eminent civilian leaders (including many whom he had jailed following the coup) and asked them to form an advisory group on the type of state—federal or unitary—that Burma should have under a new constitution. After much deliberation, the group voted for a federal structure—but its conclusions were ignored in the development of the 1974 constitution. Instead, new "ethnic" states were created (the Mon state, the Arakan state, and the Chin Special Division, which became a state; Nu had actually promised a Mon state as early as 1958). The result was in fact a highly unitary state divided into 14 geographic entities: 7 divisions representing the essentially Burman areas and 7 representing areas with heavy, often diverse, ethnic representation. Local ethnic control was a myth; in reality, the system mandated a centralized political system but in diverse geographic settings. With a unicameral National Assembly, the *Pyithu Hluttaw*, and under the leadership of the BSPP, all indigenous minorities could participate in the political process but only under rules and through institutions established by the BSPP, which in effect meant by the Burman military.

The two constitutions epitomize the debate on the nature of the Burmese state and the definition of ethnicity in Burma. One academic school considers the 1974 constitution, which downplays ethnic considerations, as far more in keeping with Burmese historical precedent than the 1947 hybrid, Westernized document. A second school maintains that in the modern world, ethnicity has become an important factor that the unitary state ignored. The next constitution must grapple with this issue again.

Scholars also question the traditional fixed definition of ethnicity, arguing that this quality is in fact a complex concept that changes over time and varies among different places and cultures. Furthermore, some observers argue that the Burmese use of ethnic terms is often spurious, since only major groups are considered, and since significant subdivisions within these groups are also ignored.

Yet the practical questions remain. Official Burmese figures (however derived—and some are patently questionable) note that in 1983 the Burmans constituted 69 percent of the population, the Shan 8.5 percent, the Karen 6.2 percent, the Arakanese 4.5 percent, the Mon 2.4 percent, the Chin 2.2 percent, the Kachin 1.4 percent, the Kayah 0.4 percent, and other indigenous groups 0.1 percent. Many important groups—the large Naga, Wa, Palaung, Lisu, and other populations—are not listed in these calculations.

The BSPP practice of nominating (and thus electing) party representatives stifled local initiative and central responsiveness to local needs. It gave rise to at least 49 highly local or ethnic party designations when the 233 political parties (subsequently 207) were registered in 1989. This seems to indicate a strong popular concern with regional and local issues, some of which may be ethnic. It is significant that in Burma Proper, the demand for local leadership seems to have become almost as great as in the minority areas.

A return to a single-party political system with subsidiary organizations controlling virtually all aspects of social and economic life seems highly unlikely, at least for some time. There are probably many in the military who would prefer to see the *tatmadaw* continue to rule directly, and others, both civilian and military, who believe that a single-party system with a strong leader is needed. But the prevailing mood is for some type of multiparty system. The population now seems cowed, but if a plan for a new single-party state were again put forward, widespread public outrage could be expected. Burma has already embarked on its choice.

How might such a system work? The SLORC, in its draft election law of March 1, 1989, and final law of June 1, 1989, stipulated that the system of township representation was inadequate. Instead, Burma would return to the British-imposed "district" system that was continued in the civilian period, but which Ne Win eliminated. The term "district" would be changed to "township zones," grouping a number of townships together. This reorganization may make for more efficient administration. Some opposition politicians have already announced that their party's candidates will be locally chosen, and thus presumably more acceptable locally. It seems likely that the NUP will do the same, although it will draw upon the previous political infrastructure of the BSPP.

There are many questions associated with a return to multiparty politics. If one or more parties are able to assume power, the strong factional tendencies that give rise to entourages and exploitation of a political pork barrel system may be especially difficult to balance under conditions of economic scarcity and deprivation. If the military stays in power while a constitution is formulated and approved, this will raise additional dire issues for that process and for the future.

Military-Civilian Relations. The critical issue in Burma's future will be the role of the military. Although the collective term "military" is used, it should by no means be construed to imply unanimity of military views, even if that group is the most cohesive institution in the state. Many in Burma now believe that many in the *tatmadaw* would prefer to return to their barracks after the besmirching of their reputation by the deaths they inflicted in 1988. However, some say, fear of retaliation against Ne Win and other leaders, and against the lower ranks who perpetrated the crimes, forces them to remain in power—as does the desire to retain their substantial perquisites.

The problem of how to cope with the end of military rule and the excesses perpetrated under previous regimes has recently faced a variety of countries. In South Korea, President Roh Tae Woo, although himself a military man and once a close associate of former President Chun Doo Hwan, is attempting to satisfy both left and right. Chun did finally apologize to the Korean people, and at this writing is living in internal exile in a Buddhist temple. In contrast, in Thailand in 1973, Generals Prapat and Thanom were allowed to leave the country after the student revolution. Syngman Rhee, Ferdinand Marcos, and Jean-Claude Duvalier were whisked away from their countries by the United States to avoid further confrontations. Argentina and Uruguay are currently facing the question of amnesty or pardons for former military leaders.

It is impossible to gauge the comparative degree of hostility toward some of the military in Burma. Given the *tatmadaw*'s continuous exhortations to the populace on the military's concern for their welfare, such animosity must be extensive, but whether it is directed toward individuals or toward the institution itself is uncertain. Meanwhile, various edicts forbid "divisive" criticism or ridicule of the *tatmadaw*. Recent rumors in Rangoon held that the Burmese were looking to the Chun model in Korea for the means to deal honorably with Ne Win. Even if not true, the rumors illustrate Burma's concern with the problem.

There is no question that any regime that comes to power will have to come to terms with the military. During the former civilian period, Ne Win was both commander of the armed forces and for a while minister of defense. It is likely that in any elected government the *tatmadaw* will minimally control the defense portfolio and, through surrogates, perhaps some other ministries, including foreign affairs, as well.

The military continues to be at the acme of the power elite. Perhaps more important for the future, it is at the social and economic pinnacle as well. It has been able to convey the opportunity to maintain this status to its children. Yet the military has been hurt by its excesses and economic failures, and perhaps also by its continuing access to the good life at times when the population was suffering. It has now lost much of the population's inherent trust. Compounding this problem, the present active-duty military is the first group not to wear the "star of independence," the battle ribbons indicating participation in the anticolonial struggle. Thus they do not enter the political fray with the cachet of their predecessors.

Both active-duty and retired military dominate the Burmese scene, although the military has only marginally expanded its personnel in the past decade (in 1988 it was estimated to number 200,000, of whom 184,000 were in the army). Casualties in the peripheral internal wars, never fully published, have been estimated by knowledgeable Burmese observers at "much higher than 5 percent" annually. Although active-duty military personnel are now forbidden to belong to any political party, retired soldiers and officers probably will participate extensively in any new political activity.

The new, more rigid class structure has produced much popular rancor. At the same time, some highly placed civilians, dependent

68

on the military and sometimes related to them, feel their status has been threatened. They feared the social and economic revolution of the summer of 1988 that, if it had succeeded, would have swept away much that they had gained. To them, it was the edge of anarchy.

As noted, the degree of unanimity among the military is unknown, but there are likely to be significant differences within it. There was, after all, an attempted coup against Ne Win in 1976 by younger officers, and a number were reportedly dismissed in 1987 for grumbling about economic conditions. These younger officers had little or no personal loyalty to Ne Win.

Further, there are several potential splits within the military based on training and function. For example, there are said to be differences between the Officer Candidate School graduates, who may have had some previous higher-level education, and those from the Defense Services Academy, whose only education took place under the rigors of a military command system. Some say there are splits between those who have risen to higher staff levels through combat and those who have done so through party or nonmilitary roles. Although there are no reported differences in political outlook or in the manner in which various military groups have treated the ethnic rebellions, it would be highly surprising if there were not real and important cleavages on these issues too.

In addition, the SLORC leadership may not be typical of the future military elite. Of 18 leaders, 10 have had only a high school education or less, 4 have had some college, and 4 have college degrees or their equivalent. Their educational level probably insulates them from more cosmopolitan views of their role, and perhaps from Burma's international needs and potential participation as well.

Since independence, the role of the military in Burma has been less to protect the state against external threats than to put down internal centrifugal tendencies—the inclination of ethnic elements to spin off into independent entities. This has colored the views of the military toward the rebellions on the periphery, rebellions that have persisted, in one case for many decades, and that in many instances are closely connected with warlordism and the drug trade. The military, at least publicly, has consistently treated the rebellions as military operations rather than political ones.

Ethnic Rebellions and Narcotics. Ethnic rebellions have become almost a permanent fixture of independent Burma. Since the Karen went into revolt in 1949, a bewildering array of groups have used ethnic designations to identify themselves with these peoples.

These ethnic groups vary. Some, such as the Karen, have eschewed the drug trade. Others, such as various Shan groups, are deeply involved in this lucrative business. Some rebellions have patent religious motivations, such as that of Muslims in Arakan. Others, including those led by some Christian-oriented groups, are less unified around a single religious concept.

The Karen insurrection has existed for four decades and may be the oldest sustained rebellion in the world; the impetus for many of the others came with the 1962 military coup and the consequent destruction of local autonomy. In some cases, rebellions were said to have been related to the elimination of the traditional rights of the *sawbwas* in 1959 and the cessation of the legal opium trade that same year, both accomplished under the military caretaker government. Some Shan would deny this and link their rebellion to the collapse of the economy and the atrocities of the Burma army. The issue is further clouded by the fact that heroin traffic developed at about the same time, making the opium trade vastly more financially rewarding.

The rebellions are complicated by other illegal activities. Some are supported by taxes on the smuggling trade that passes through the rebels' region. The Karen, for example, charge a 5 percent *ad valorem* transit tax on these goods. The Kachin themselves smuggle jade, the Arakanese, rice.

Some rebels had early demanded independence from Burma, whereas others called for U.N. trusteeship. These demands have now been dropped, and the cry instead is for some sort of a federal system within a Union of Burma. Yet the outward orientation of the rebellions, including their economic links with the world beyond Burma, have made them particularly threatening to the Burmans. Some rebellions have at various periods been covertly supported by foreign governments (the Thai supported Nu and his revolt in the 1970s; the Chinese supported the Burma Communist Party for many years under the pretext that party-to-party relations were different from diplomatic relations). Some rebellions, such as those of the Naga and the Chin, supported internal revolts in India. The little that was reported in the international press on Burma seemed to the Burmese government to be unduly concentrated on the rebellions and minority issues.

Thus there have been valid reasons for the Burman concern about ethnic issues and the potential splintering of the state, as well as valid minority worries about the Burman role and the army. Although Ne Win on two occasions attempted to negotiate with the rebels, he was generally unsuccessful. As recently as July 1989, the military indicated that it was not prepared to negotiate again with the minority rebels. But the economic limitations of the current government, the relatively static size of the military and its low technological capacity, the remoteness of the regions, and the size of the rebellious forces all preclude a military solution, although increased military pressure is now evident against the Karen. At the same time, the rebellions cannot topple the state; they can only bleed it slowly, delaying the realization of its economic potential and political unity. The government admits to spending 25 percent of its budget on defense, but the figure is likely to be closer to 40 percent. Some say 80 percent of earned foreign exchange goes for armaments.

In addition to the ethnic rebellions have been those of the Burma Communist Party and the former *Kuomintang* (Chinese Nationalist forces). The BCP self-destructed in April 1989. It had conducted its own reformation—a symbolic, not actual, "long march"—in 1975 after its defeat in the mountains of central Burma, regrouping in the vast Wa state (part of the Shan state) on the Chinese border. Its recruits were largely minority, and its leadership was also ethnically diffuse. In past negotiations with the Burmese government the BCP had called for the retention of its own administration and military within its areas, a call strengthened by its having the largest single rebel military force in Burma (perhaps 15,000 at the time). The BCP was originally vehemently against the opium trade, but when Beijing's economic support diminished, it was forced to take part in it to support its rebellion. The BCP was the only ideologically committed force in rebellion.

The remnants of the *Kuomintang*, after their defeat by the Chinese communists in 1950, retreated into Burma (in 1644 Ming forces did the same), where they were clandestinely assisted by the United States and Taiwan. Although some were evacuated to Taiwan in the mid-1950s, others remained (there are many in northern Thailand as well), and they too have entered the opium trade. Thus parts of Burma are steeped in what might be called ethnic warlordism.

The opium/heroin trade is very profitable, mostly to the middlemen, refiners, and traffickers; much less so to the producers of the opium poppy, who are marginal farmers. This trade is also eminently suited to the region. It is climatically appropriate, labor-intensive, high in value, and easy to transport. For all of these reasons, efforts to replace it have failed. The "Golden Triangle," including northeastern Burma, northwestern Laos, and northern Thailand, is infamous, and Burma is by far the largest producer in the region, growing perhaps 75 percent of the total regional volume of opium.

Production figures in Burma vary annually, influenced by the weather and the degree of government control over the region, the latter being tenuous at best. The estimates for 1987–88 show some 1,300 tons of raw opium produced in Burma, about double the estimates of several years ago, which American officials feel were undercounted. A decade ago the estimates of total production were 300 tons. Some estimates place Burmese 1989 production at 2,000 tons. The reasons for this increase, aside from good weather, are disputed, although continuing demand is the most obvious. The opium in its raw and refined states is now exported through all of Burma's neighbors, as well as through Burma itself, and many charge that high officials in these countries personally benefit. The financing of rebellions provides a local stimulus to the trade, as does a tradition of warlordism. Some argue that aerial spraying by the Burmese army (with U.S. assistance) has cut the crop. Others maintain that the spraying has caused the producers to expand production to protect their investments. The halt to such assistance with the closure of the U.S. foreign assistance program in September 1989 may again affect production.

The traditional route for smuggling the refined heroin went through Thailand to the United States and Europe. There has now been extensive diversification of the traffic; some is said to go to Hong Kong by sea as well as through China; some through India; some to Bombay and Europe via Bangladesh; and some by sea from Burma (via the port of Moulmein) to Penang and Singapore.

U.S. concern with this traffic has been great and is shared by the Burmese, who have seen a growing internal addiction problem. About half of the U.S. economic assistance of US$15 million annually to Burma was to support antinarcotics programs. Most U.S. assistance since 1985 has been directed to eliminating opium production through interdiction equipment and on-ground and aerial spraying. The chemical 2.4D has been used, which has raised environmental concerns. In the late 1970s, some congressional staff suggested that the United States buy and burn the total crop, an action that would have involved the United States in supplying funds to the rebels and in providing an assured market for any future production. In September 1989 the Burmese government claimed to have destroyed 200,000 acres of opium between 1975 and 1988.

To control the opium/heroin production and traffic would require government control over a region that has eluded effective administration by any Burmese regime. Crop substitution efforts, only partly successful at best worldwide, depend on rural infrastructure such as roads and markets. Since these are lacking in the affected regions, this strategy is unlikely to work in Burma any time soon. The suppression of this trade will depend on some solution to the minority issues, but it is unlikely that even this would be sufficient to eliminate it.

In 1963 the Burmese government was said to have collaborated with certain of the drug lords by incorporating them as recognized local militia (KKY) and protecting their opium traffic, in return for which the KKY would assure state control over local areas by fighting the BCP. Khun Sa, the best known and strongest leader of the opium trade, has been rumored to have worked with the Burmese government recently, as well as with individual military commanders, and with the *Kuomintang* in the earlier period. Secret negotiations with the BCP remnants in late 1989 followed a well-established pattern: if rebellions cannot be quashed, coopt them.

The Economy—Central Planning, Local Initiative, and Minority Participation. The administrative centralization of power has strongly affected the Burmese economy. In the civilian period, some minority groups, especially the Shan, did not believe that they received sufficient benefits from the center, either through subsidies or foreign aid. Some wished to negotiate directly with foreign organizations for aid, and this theme has again appeared as the 1990 elections approach.

There is little question that the local capacity to plan—always weak—was completely eliminated under the military. The military was even unable to make the regional colleges work effectively. However, the state has not been able to suppress local entrepreneurship, most evident in smuggling, and now in the regularized and black-market trade with China. Stifled local initiative, with few legal outlets, has found its way into illegal activities. One of the issues facing a new administration in Burma will be how to tap into such advantageous endeavors and encourage the economy and profit from its growth without reducing the authority of the state by overtly or covertly condoning extralegal economic activities.

Burma will also have to come to terms with the likely resurgence of "foreign" minorities under a liberalized economic structure that encourages the private sector. In a sense here as well the choice has already been made, for if the Burmese open the private sector, resident Chinese and Indian businessmen will take advantage of their previous experience and their networks of overseas credit and business contacts. Even if the official financial institutions expand to provide private credit these informal but highly effective "foreign" credit systems will probably come into play, either independently or through Burmese middlemen. On September 4, 1989, the Myanma (sic) Investment and Commercial Bank opened. It will serve foreign investors and joint ventures by providing, in addition to the usual banking facilities, project appraisal, project supervision, and advice. This still leaves the Burmese private sector isolated. Beginning down the path toward liberalization, a direction that was economically necessary, will inevitably create other problems.

When Thailand, with World Bank advice, opted in 1959 for a liberal economic development program featuring the private sector, it in effect decided to include its resident Chinese, hitherto important but unintegrated. More than any other Asian nation with a Chinese minority, Thailand has successfully integrated its Chinese into the dominant culture, fusing all bureaucratic, military, and entrepreneurial communities into a vibrant, interdependent whole. Should Burma wish to pursue that liberal economic model, the explicit integration of its much smaller Chinese community over the next generation could be a plausible strategy or a necessary result. The emerging Burmese middle class may well be made up of resident Chinese and former smugglers.

Burma must also come to grips with its public sector—the State Economic Enterprises. Organized under 23 corporations (now renamed "enterprises"), they have controlled most of Burma's larger productive establishments. These companies have been run as bureaucracies, staffed at the top by military or party officials without management or economic training, and stifled by politics. Employees could not be fired, price adjustments were slow and cumbersome to approve, and many of the industries were unsuited to Burmese conditions. Their economic efficiency was predicated, for example, on 24-hour production when in fact they only operate for 8 hours a day. Some corporations were prestige or peripheral projects, and since they were assisted by low-interest foreign loans, their economic efficiency was viewed as irrelevant. Feasibility studies for these projects were often omitted, or such studies were changed to suit and justify the whims of the leadership. Raw materials or spare parts often could not be purchased for lack of priority interest in assigning foreign exchange. Accordingly, as foreign debt grew to pay for many of these industries, internal debt also grew. And foreign donors participated in this charade.

The government inadvertently made the situation even worse. Needing to supply diminishing goods to its rising population, the government quietly encouraged the smuggling trade. The largest market for such goods in Rangoon was actually set up and taxed by the city. The result was that even relatively efficient Burmese factories could not compete with imported Chinese, Indian, or Bangladeshi products for price or quality. There are, therefore, serious questions about whether Burmese industry in the foreseeable future will have the skills, economies of scale, or incentives to produce light industrial products efficiently. The government may have sacrificed the future of its industry for short-term political gain.

Turning off the public-sector spigot will mean the firing of large numbers of workers, the sale or lease of factories to private investors, and perhaps internal political problems as well. Insofar as some factories can be reoriented toward manufacturing exports under foreign management, they may prove successful. But this would require the government to relinquish many of its interests, which it might find difficult to do.

Cultural Diversity and National Unity. Since independence, the state has enshrined in every constitution the rights of minorities to practice their cultures. Theoretically, the government encourages cultural diversity. Yet in fact, all the systems in Burma that allow growth, development, and mobility are those dominated by the Burman cultural tradition.

This situation is not surprising, but it has led to considerable local resentment. Minority cultures and languages are relegated to one's home and cannot be used for other than local purposes. Education is in Burmese; the symbols of the state and the deployment of power are Burman. Two decades ago, the Shan of the Shan state looked with envy on the Shan-language primary school textbooks of the Xishuangbanna Autonomous Region of Yunnan province in the People's Republic of China. "The Burmese Way to Socialism" might more accurately be termed "The Burman Way to Socialism," because it reflects Burman cultural, political, and nationalistic norms.

The search for national unity, so important in Burma under all administrations and reflected in the very terminology of the state, is still ineffectual. For the past quarter-century, unity has been seen to require an iron hand—uniformity rather than tolerance and flexibility. A new administration may wish to reconsider this approach, but to make such a change will require acceptance by the military.

There is a sense so far that to achieve national unity, conformity is required. In May 1989 General Saw Maung announced a new program to chronicle modern Burmese history and demonstrate, among other things, the correctness of the military's intervention in

75

state affairs and the proper view of history. That the government should go to such lengths indicates that diversity of opinion on critical issues is not yet regarded as an asset, even though the official chronicling of history is in the dynastic tradition. Unity is still imposed from the center, rather than rising voluntarily from common interests. If, however, unity cannot be internally generated, it may be promoted by playing on people's fears of foreign domination, uniting the state not for common interests but against common enemies.

Burma and the World

Neutralism, Commerce, and Technology. Burma has been known as the neutralist nation *par excellence.* Thant became secretary-general of the United Nations not because of any particular qualifications, but because he came from a country that could be depended upon to walk a tightrope between East and West. And in fact, Burma has scrupulously adhered to that role. It was the first noncommunist country to recognize the People's Republic of China; it supported the U.N. action in Korea; it was at the Bandung Conference; and it was in the Non-Aligned Movement until 1979, when it walked out of the meeting in Havana because it felt that the position of the conference had moved too close to the Soviet Union. In addition, Burma stopped the U.S. economic assistance program twice (although on the first occasion it paid for continued American economic planning assistance with its own funds); cut off diplomatic relations with China in 1967 over local problems spawned by the Cultural Revolution; insisted on paying for Soviet aid with rice; and offered Rangoon as a site to negotiate the end of the Vietnam War. Although Burma's relations with its neighbors have been peaceful and border agreements have been made with all of them, Burma has refused to join any blocs, neither ASEAN or the earlier SEATO to the east, nor South Asian groupings to the west.

Burma has also had a special relationship with China, which it has long feared because of China's massive population and past history (China destroyed the Burmese capital of Pagan in 1287 and invaded Burma on several occasions thereafter). Sun Yat-Sen regarded Burma as part of the Chinese sphere. Modern Chinese maps have in the postwar period included northern Burma in China's territory, and the Burmese were fearful that Chinese communist forces might pursue the *Kuomintang* into Burma and take over territory on that pretext. On the other side, the Chinese supported the rebel Burma Communist Party and in March 1971 started a clandestine liberation radio station beamed at Burma and operated from Yunnan province. When the BCP leaders were evicted by the Wa in April 1989, they retreated into China.

On the other hand, Burmese delegations, often including Ne Win, went to Beijing for friendly visits, and the Chinese reciprocated by going to Rangoon. The Burmese refer to the Chinese as *paukhpaw*, or kin. Burma collaborated with the Chinese military, who were quietly allowed across the border to fight against the *Kuomintang* and in more recent times to clear the trade routes.

During the civilian period, Prime Minister Nu encouraged outside contacts. State scholars were sent abroad for training, while foreign researchers were allowed into Burma. Nu was personally on good terms with a wide range of foreign dignitaries, and Burma was well represented at international conferences.

Then, following the 1962 coup and until the late 1970s, the military government reinterpreted Burma's neutrality as isolationism. It cut Burma off from the outside world by allowing few Burmese out, and almost no foreigners in, except for casual tourists, who were allowed to visit for short periods only (at first, 24 hours; then, 72 hours; later, a week; and more recently, two weeks). Whereas Thailand had more than 4 million tourists in 1986 and Nepal had approximately 400,000, Burma had only about 40,000. Burma was represented at few international meetings, and diplomats' travel within Burma was unnecessarily restricted even in secure areas. The military generally controlled access and information and treated those Burmese who had foreign experience or connections with suspicion. Burmese officials had to report all contact with foreigners and for long periods were not allowed to visit their homes. The intelligence network also required urban bloc or village party leaders to report all Burmese visitors to their areas.

Burma faced a dilemma. As an exporter of primary products, it had to trade to survive. But it had little foreign economic intelligence capacity and did not encourage its officials to develop the knowledge of foreign markets that might have improved Burmese exports and the prices Burma received for them. As its neighbors expanded their economic liberalization, Burma's policies became even more anachronistic. With restricted information, Burma often misinterpreted the actions of foreign powers. When it did open itself to increased foreign contacts through foreign economic assistance programs that sent Burmese abroad for training, and when it allowed foreign journalists in for short visits and let more Burmese emigrate, the door was still only half open; the deep-rooted anxieties about foreign exposure were still apparent.

The sources of these attitudes are varied. They include the fact that foreign nations have decried Burmese neutrality; that the Burmese depend on foreign prices—kept artificially low from a Burmese perspective—for their commodities; and that even Burma's internal economy has in large part been controlled by foreigners for much of its modern history.

Although the Burmese government has reason for its fears, it has magnified them into xenophobia to cover its own errors. For example, close associates of Ne Win have blamed Burma's economic troubles on foreign discrimination because of Burma's neutrality. In addition, the military's fear of criticism has led the Burmese to refuse to allow foreigners to scrutinize economic policies. Thus in 1988 and 1989 the government of Burma refused to have dealings with the International Monetary Fund, perhaps because of concern lest the errors of subordinates be conveyed to its leader and on account of the requirement to allow IMF surveillance of the economy.

Yet the world has changed. Burma could be isolated in 1962; it cannot be today. Anyone overseas can direct-dial a cabinet minister or a leader of the opposition. Banned books can be imported on a single computer disc. Photocopying machines abound in urban areas, and have, for example, clandestinely reproduced Brigadier Aung Gyi's critical letters to Ne Win, for which there was a substantial demand and a relatively high price. International radio news programs are quite popular in Burma and often report local events ignored by the government-controlled media. In fact, urban Burmese are aware of much that is happening abroad.

The government has not yet completely recognized this. It is aware that it badly needs new technology for Burma's vital industries, such as oil, mining, and agriculture. It is prepared to train students and staff overseas in some of these fields. The government also recognizes that tourism can be a major foreign exchange earner (it is now Thailand's greatest source), although it specifically rejects Rangoon's becoming another Bangkok. Many believe that too great and too fast an influx of foreign ideas or people will lead to corruption of the idealized primal state of traditional Burma, which they hope to preserve.

In a sense, the Burmese leadership is attempting to deal with the issues of development as China (unsuccessfully) and Japan (successfully) did in the latter part of the 19th century. It recognizes that Burma needs technology, but it wants to keep this need confined to technical areas, a kind of Burmese "self-strengthening" movement, preserving Burma's unique, pristine cultural context. For this reason, Ne Win was fearful of the incursion of foreign television. He personally destroyed the drum of a Western-style orchestra that annoyed him and banned the international pop musical culture, but now the ease of reproducing cassette tapes has made such efforts pointless.

Nor can other technological change be easily channeled. Exposure to the outside world will not be contained within government-prescribed parameters. How the government deals with this issue will be an important component in the rate of change in Burma and its internal and external credibility.

The dire economic straits in which Burma presently finds itself will hasten the process of opening to the outside. The need for quick, effective joint ventures with foreign firms and for an expanding private sector will mean more foreign businesspeople in Burma, more economic and social infrastructure supporting their presence, more technical assistance, more jobs, and more personal contact between Burmese and the outside world. The state has agreed that the management of many types of joint venture will have to remain in foreign hands for at least five years, thus increasing the number of foreigners in Burma. Their influence will expand, with concomitant effects on the society.

The informal trade will also contribute to the foreign presence. No longer required to have visas or passports, Chinese now are quite common in Mandalay and elsewhere. As the Burmese expand their open-border system to include Thailand, more Thais are expected in Lower Burma as well.

Out of necessity, Burma has agreed to enter the world, but it has attempted to do so on its own restrictive terms. Burmese will disapprove as cultural norms are violated by foreigners and their presence induces inflation in housing and other commodities. The Burmese government has attempted in the past to insulate its population from these effects, but that will be increasingly difficult. Burma has already made the choice for more contact. It may not, however, have grasped the full implications of that decision.

Burma in Asia. Burma has maintained friendly relations with all of its neighbors. Its relations with Thailand in particular have vastly improved since September 1988. The reasons spring from the perceived interests of both countries.

Thailand is now witnessing a substantial, sustained rate of economic growth. With a strong military presence within its civilian government, Thailand is assuming a dominant position in the Southeast Asian mainland. It supports the "Golden Chersonese" principle, a reinvigoration of the classic description of mainland Southeast Asia as the Golden Peninsula—but now to be led by Thailand. In spite of internal Thai debate and rivalries between Thai military and civilians, and between ministries and the political parties and individuals that control them, Thailand is bent on assuming a more important role in peninsular Southeast Asia. Much of that focus relates to changes in Indochina, especially Cambodia, but Burma is also an essential part of that picture.

The improvements in Thai-Burmese relations since September 1988 are remarkable, even if some of the alleged moves were too discreet to be verified. The changes are even more noteworthy because of the traditional enmity between the two states, in spite of the modern charade of courtesy. Thailand has harbored Burmese rebels, including Nu, and it received two of the Burmese Shan states from Japan in return for its World War II collaboration, though these were later returned. The Thai still remember the Burmese sack of their capital, Ayutthaya, in 1767, but since the Burmese coup of 1988 they have officially downplayed that event in Thai government tourist publications.

There is a persistent rumor that in September 1988, about a week before the coup, General Saw Maung as chief-of-staff of the *tatmadaw* secretly flew to Chiangmai and there met General Chavalit, supreme commander of the Thai armed forces. Saw Maung is said to have told Chavalit that Burma was descending into anarchy, from which only the communists would benefit. Therefore, at some appropriate time, the Burmese *tatmadaw* were going to launch a coup to support the failing regime, and it was in Thai interests that this be done. If this scenario is correct, the coup was planned in advance, though the date was determined by local events in Burma. This rumor cannot be verified, but it is a plausible beginning to today's closer Burmo-Thai relationship.

After the coup, sometime in November, the Thai bureaucracy realized that Chavalit was planning to visit Burma in December. To preempt that move, the Thai deputy foreign minister announced plans to visit Rangoon. The strong public outcry in Thailand against such a trip was prompted by the Burmese military's human rights abuses and by international reporting on the Burmese students who had fled into Thailand and the border region. The deputy foreign minister's trip was canceled, but General Chavalit and a large entourage arrived in Rangoon on December 14, 1988. During that visit, agreement seemed to have been reached on at least two items: repatriation of Burmese students and Thai investment in exploitation of Burma's natural resources.

With Thai approval, Burmese military aircraft flew on several occasions to Tak and brought back some three hundred Burmese students. Some no doubt went voluntarily, but there are rumors that
some were forced to return, and that a bounty was offered in Thailand for their identification. It was at the December meeting that
the stage was also set for Thai involvement in the Burmese economic revitalization program through fishing and teak agreements.

These agreements were followed by a veritable barrage of visits
by the Thai. The minister of agriculture came, as did other bureaucratic, military, and academic delegations. Burmese military leaders
also visited Thailand. Thailand opened a commercial section in its
embassy in Rangoon for the first time, and negotiations on other
deals were reported to have taken place as well. The Thai deputy
prime minister also came to Burma eventually, as did other subca-
binet officials.

The new Thai role in the region was spelled out by the Thai
prime minister, who delivered an *aide-mémoire* to President Bush at
Emperor Hirohito's funeral in Tokyo on February 25, 1989. In it,
the Thai prime minister called for greater U.S. and Thai cooper-
ation in improving trade and diplomatic relations with both Indochina and Burma. The Thai offered to mediate the Burmese civil
wars, an offer that the Burmese refused. There are also rumors that
the Thai military—perhaps carrying out its own foreign policy—has
allowed Burmese troops to cross into Thailand on more than one
occasion to attack Karen bases from the rear, thus freeing the trade
routes through which the Thai could get teak from Burmese territory under their agreements. The Thai military is in fact guarantee-
ing the profits of the Thai concessionaires in Burma.

To the Thai government, these initiatives are important examples
of Thailand's greater role in the region. They are also important indications of the Thai military's view of its own importance in shap-
ing Burmese internal and foreign policy. In this context, Thailand
did not want to lose the Burma market to the increasing China
trade. Yet there is also evidence that some Burmese dissidents in
Thailand are under the protection of important Thai officials, but
whether this is coordinated Thai policy or merely the action of se-
lect groups is unclear.

From the perspective of the Burmese government, the Thai relationship provides immediate economic benefits as well as diplomatic prestige and legitimacy. It also diffuses any possible Thai
support for the rebel movements back and forth across the Thailand-Burma border. This newly intense relationship is thus in the
short-range interest of the present government. The relationship

will likely grow as Burma reaches formal agreement with Thailand to open its borders and legitimize its trade, thus gaining custom duties while depriving the Karen and Mon rebels of some of their income. Informally, this already seems to have occurred.

The Chinese and Burmese have conceived of their relationship as close, virtually kin, in spite of China's previous support of the BCP. In the early period of Burmese independence, there were also minor border disputes, such as the moving of boundary pillars back and forth across a strategic road. The military finally negotiated the border agreement during the caretaker government. The Chinese may have viewed an agreement with Burma as protection of their eastern flank in their territorial disputes with India near the Burma border, across which tribal peoples migrated at will. China has provided US$64 million for a variety of projects over the years, and the Chinese and Burmese have had agreements on the purchase of rice. Significantly, a Burmese military delegation visited China in October 1989 to study the Chinese management of media and information.

Although diplomatic relations and economic assistance indicate a close tie, the most important element has been the burgeoning informal and then formal trade between Burma and China. This trade has been the single most important support for a faltering Burmese economy. Through a highly organized and widespread economic reporting network, the Chinese are able to monitor both Burmese production and foreign smuggled imports and thus to indicate to the Chinese in Yunnan which commodities are in short supply and where demand is high. For example, a type of Burmese *longyi* (sarong) of a particular design smuggled from Madras is now imported from China. How much of the Yunnan industrial product is destined for the Burmese market is unknown, but some two thousand items from all over China are admittedly sent to Burma, which in turn sells almost any local primary product to China.

Part of this economic equation results from very low Burmese productivity and quality and uneconomic production scales. But some of it is a result of poor producer-pricing policies in Burma. For example, crude rubber from the south is supposed to be sold to the state for K3 per pound, but private middlemen will pay K10. And even with transport costs and payoffs en route to the northern border totaling an additional K10, the rubber is sold there for K30.

Banking facilities, hotels, and godowns are said to be operating on both sides of the border, and the Ministry of Construction in Burma is supposed to have improved the road from the railhead at Lashio to the border at Muse, the route of the famous Burma Road of World War II. Although other "ports" are also open (including Namhkam), this is the most convenient and largest. From the Burmese viewpoint, a posting to any one of the many Burmese bureaucratic or military jobs in the region is a plum, for which one may have to bribe.

The volume of trade is said to total US$1.5 billion a year, although the Burmese official estimate of December 1988 was only US$300 million. It is likely that the Burmese government can monitor only a fraction of the trade.

The results of the China trade are both short- and long-term. Northern Burma, especially Mandalay, Lashio, and Maymyo, are booming, with rising land prices and a spurt of private housing construction. The money that is being made from these activities may well find its way into future private-sector investment. Much of that money is, of course, illegal, and much is probably in the hands of the Chinese community in Burma. Thus it will likely give the Chinese an even more important position in the Burmese economy than the strong one they already have.

Of even more permanent significance is the trade's likely effect on the Burmese economy, in both state and private sectors. Chinese industrial economies of scale, wage rates, and the quality, design, and durability of their products will undercut the overall Burmese capacity to produce consumer goods at competitive prices, and it will be exceedingly difficult for either the State Economic Enterprises or private-sector producers to match Chinese products. Yet Burma's vested interests in this trade, and in the extracurricular incomes associated with it, are so great that it is unlikely that any government will be able to suppress it. China is not the only country supplying Burma with consumer goods, but it has become the largest and most diversified supplier.

Interestingly, the Chinese are more acceptable to the Burmese on ethnic and religious grounds than are any of the inhabitants of the subcontinent. Chinese-style Buddhist shrines can be seen interspersed among Burmese ones, although the Buddhism of each is from a different school. Intermarriage is not infrequent. The subcontinent, however, is regarded with suspicion, especially Muslim states because of the Muslim minority in Arakan and a history from the prewar period of communal tension in times of economic hardship. There are continuous virulent rumors among the Burmans of Muslim activities designed to destroy the Burman social and religious fabric and to convert the Buddhist faithful, especially Burman women. These rumors are important for the stereotypes they perpetuate, but the informal trading patterns are important as well. India, although geographically distant from major trading areas of Burma, is actually able to export goods into central Burma conveniently and cheaply through the town of Tamu and down the Mu and Chindwin rivers into the Irrawaddy. This route has also become a prime source for the chemicals necessary to convert opium into heroin. Bangladesh may be the largest illegal importer of Burmese rice; the sea route there is inexpensive and easy for bulk goods such as paddy. But Burma signed a Border Trade Agreement as well as a General Trade Agreement on June 1, 1989, involving US$20 million in countertrade. In addition, there is joint cooperation on a K20 million prawn project.

Singapore has been the entrepôt for Burma as well as for much of the region. Through or from Singapore have come earlier (unadmitted) oil imports and military equipment (made in or shipped through Singapore). Both sides have denied this trade, but it has been extensively reported in the press. Singapore firms now have two joint ventures with the Burmese government.

The Republic of Korea has also begun to assume a more important role in Burmese affairs. Relations have been close since the Rangoon bombing of 1983, in which 17 South Korean and 4 Burmese senior officials were assassinated at the Aung San memorial by North Korean agents. Burma "derecognized" North Korea after the incident, for not only were these deaths a violation of international law, they were a direct insult to Ne Win, who was host to Korean president Chun Doo Hwan. In the spring of 1989 Burma announced the opening of its embassy in Seoul. (South Korea had had an embassy in Rangoon since 1975.)

South Korea has engaged in multilateral aid projects in Burma, such as the Kinde Dam (Hyundai Construction). Daewoo Company, which has an office in Rangoon, operates a blouse assembly plant outside Rangoon employing 1,300 Burmese and opened a department store in Rangoon in July 1989. It also has a textile mill and plans to invest some US$20 million to expand a copper mining venture previously supported by Yugoslavia. Korean vessels have been licensed to fish in Burmese waters. There have also been rumors that Korea has been supplying arms to the Burmese military. In October 1989 Korea's Yukong Oil Company signed an agreement with the Burmese government for onshore oil exploration in the Chindwin basin. Under it, Yukong will supply US$70 million over 5 years. There will be a period of exploration for 3 to 5 years, followed by 25 years of production during which the profits will be shared, with 30 percent going to the Koreans and 70 percent to the Burmese government. South Korea has clearly attempted to move into segments of the economic vacuum in Burma, yet Burma's exports to Korea were only US$5.4 million in 1987.

Although Burma has no formal diplomatic relations with Taiwan, the large surpluses in that state have prompted Taiwan Chinese to look to Southeast Asia for investment opportunities, especially to the Philippines, Thailand, and Indonesia. But there are some thirty thousand Sino-Burmese in Taiwan, many of whom retain an involvement in or curiosity about Burmese economic affairs. Some have explicitly indicated interest in business possibilities in Burma. In spite of the absence of diplomatic relations, a Taiwanese commercial mission was said to have visited Burma in 1989. Taiwanese funds will likely find their way into Burmese ventures through the overseas Chinese communities in both Thailand and Singapore.

Since the early 1950s Japan has been Burma's primary support. The Japanese role in the Burmese economy has been paramount since the end of World War II. It began with reparations, under which Japan engaged in a large number of projects, the most important of which was the Lawpida hydroelectric project that supplied power to much of the country. Japan also provided Burma with producer and consumer goods that established a continuing market for Japanese products. And during the dark economic era of most of the 1960s, the Burmese government might have collapsed without Japanese assistance.

In the late 1970s Japanese assistance went up some tenfold, from about US$20 million annually in the 1960s to about US$200 million, or almost half of all Burma's foreign support. There may have been complex reasons for such assistance: Japanese guilt about the war (Burma was the most devastated nation in Asia aside from Japan itself); the economic potential of Burma, especially as a supplier of oil; the pressures in Japan to increase foreign aid; Japanese business interests; Burmese poverty; and the special relationship the Japanese had with Ne Win from the early 1940s, when they trained him to fight against the British. During the caretaker government, Ne Win even talked about importing Japanese farm labor to show the Burmese how to farm better in the sparsely populated Mu Valley in the Sagaing division. From all the diplomatic corps, only the Japanese ambassador had continuing access to Ne Win.

That Japan put pressure on the Burmese government in April 1988 to reform its economic policies was a major event for both nations: Japan had previously avoided such policy discussions with any aid recipient, and Burma had firmly prevented all foreign governments from attempting to force policy changes. The degradation of Burma's economy forced this unique measure, which may have

85

been the final element in prompting Ne Win to begin some changes that he had earlier recognized were necessary. Although the cumulative level of Japanese assistance including war reparations is difficult to calculate, it must be at least US$3 billion, with Burma one of the highest national recipients, perhaps receiving the largest amount on a per capita basis. That assistance, however, dropped from US$244 million in 1986 to US$165 million in 1987 because of growing concern about Burma's economic policies.

It is highly unlikely that Japan's predominant position in Burma will decline in the near term. No other nation can supply Burma's foreign exchange needs to the same degree. Japanese aid is politically acceptable in Burma, since Japan is seen as a power without territorial or hegemonic ambitions. The balance of trade between Japan and Burma is highly skewed because of the commodities shipped to Burma under the aid program. Although Burma officially exported US$31.5 million in goods to Japan in 1987 (less than to a number of other countries such as China, Singapore, and Thailand), it imported US$195.5 million in products from Japan.

For the present, Japan's economic influence, however pervasive, does not seem threatening to the Burmese. In October 1989 Japan sent an economic mission to Burma, which the Burmese apparently hoped would signal the expansion of the assistance that had been truncated following the coup. This did not prove to be the case; the Japanese apparently were awaiting the results of both the planned elections and the economic reforms. Whether a new generation of Burmese leaders in the post–Ne Win era will turn to Japan with the same alacrity that he did is uncertain, but Japanese assistance will likely remain essential to Burma.

Burma has avoided joining regional blocs in order to protect its neutrality. It might become more interested in such alliances if the economic rewards were immediate and sufficiently lucrative, but the prospects are still unlikely. Nevertheless, some opposition figures consider that Burma might do well to join either ASEAN or the South Asia group (SAARC), under the naive impression that other countries in the same bloc would take action against the Burmese military should the latter attempt a coup against an elected government. Such thinking indicates the degree to which many educated Burmese have been isolated from outside reality.

Regional Rivalries in Burma. For a quarter-century, Burma has been internationally quiescent in spite of internal turmoil and incessant insurrections. Its neighbors have all maintained the proper formal relations with Burma's government, despite the fact that they may have also supported various opposition groups. Except for major-power interest in using Burma as a site from which to watch the Sino-Soviet dispute, Burma was of marginal interest to most countries. It last figured on the regional scene, and then only peripherally, as a flanking factor in the northeast quadrant of the Sino-Indian War of the early 1960s.

But a subtle change in interest in Burma has developed as the powers in the region have begun to compete with one another there. The initial impetus for this rivalry seems to have been economic, but its strategic implications are apparent to the participants.

This change may plausibly be traced to the rise of Chinese economic power in Burma, first from the extensive smuggling trade already discussed, and then from its more recent regularization. Thailand and India have both reacted to Chinese economic penetration with considerable, if unarticulated, concern. Thailand's overtures to Burma are not only the product of Thailand's economic advances or of its military's camaraderie with Burma's military leadership, but also clearly an attempt to prevent Chinese economic domination of Burma, which would entail substantial national, institutional, and personal losses to the Thai leadership. For the last three decades Thailand's policy was to insulate a leftist regime in Rangoon from Thailand by tacit support of the diverse Burmese rebels along the Thailand-Burma border. The Thai now see an opportunity to increase their economic position with investment in Burma, and to try to hold a major share of the informal trade between the two countries. A Burma dominated by even a friendly China would be a threat to Thailand.

India's interests in the region have also increased. Delhi's role in Sri Lanka, the Maldives, and Nepal, and the buildup of Indian naval capacity in the Andamans and the Bay of Bengal have not gone unnoticed; less obvious has been India's renewed interest in Burma. All-India Radio has been Burma's severest international critic and has spurred the Burmese government to many direct and indirect anti-Indian statements. On September 14, 1989, All-India Radio announced a new program in Burmese, *Pyithu Athan*, the "Voice of the People," which would explain the "real" situation in Burma where the authorities "are power-crazed and blind to the realities because of their present hold on administrative power." Smuggling to Burma via India has increased. The most powerful motive for Indian attention is the specter of a Burma economically controlled by China, which would be anathema to Indian strategic interests in the region.

There are indications that India has materially assisted the Chin (Zo) and Naga rebels and has even supported their movements within Burma. Former prime minister Rajiv Gandhi is said to have met with Kachin leader Brang Sang. This interest has been complicated by the claim of Karen rebels that they have captured Pakistani-made weapons from Burmese troops. At the same time, continuing Bangladeshi support to Muslim insurgents in Arakan and a heritage of previous refugees (in 1978 some two hundred thousand Muslim refugees fled Burma for Bangladesh, to return later under U.N. auspices) make for a potentially volatile situation.

As Burma enters the world economic scene, these rivalries can be expected to increase. They will be augmented by Burma's strategic location at the head of the Bay of Bengal and its considerable natural resource potential. A neutral Burma may be acceptable to each of the regional powers, but a Burma under any single nation's economic or political domination might be considered destabilizing. Burma will have to tread a very fine line in its future economic and diplomatic relations in the region.

Burma and the United States. The U.S. relationship with Burma has been checkered. As secretary of state, John Foster Dulles regarded Burmese neutrality in the cold war as anathema. The United States covertly supported the Chinese *Kuomintang* troops in Burma. During the acrimonious Sino-Soviet split, Rangoon was an ideal point from which to watch both nations interacting in a Third World setting. Later, U.S. interests in Burma centered on reducing the supply of Asian narcotics flooding the American market.

In 1989, U.S. motives remain similar, but with some shifts. Stemming the narcotics trade is still a primary objective, and the United States has in the past supplied Burma with police and aircraft equipment to that end. However, since the narcotics are grown in ethnic insurgent areas, it is virtually impossible to prevent the equipment from being used for anti-insurgent actions as well. When the Karen rebels, who do not grow or traffic in opium, shot down a U.S.-supplied helicopter, the incident was embarrassing to both the United States and Burma. Private reports from knowledgeable Burmese indicate that this misuse is not infrequent. In 1988, the antinarcotics program cost about US$7 million. Between 1958 and 1971, the United States supplied Burma with about US$85 million in military (police) equipment and training. U.S. economic assistance, stopped twice during the 1970s, was reactivated in 1979.

The United States has also been interested in the problem of Burma's poverty and its economic development potential. U.S. economic assistance (in addition to the antidrug program) was about

US$7 million to US$9 million a year during its final three or four years. Concentrated in training, health, and agricultural production of oil seeds, U.S. aid was small but significant. With the military coup, all U.S. economic assistance was halted pending a movement toward democracy and improved human rights.

The poverty of Burma has precluded significant U.S. government interest in that country as a market for U.S. products, but Burma's vast underutilized natural resources have proven to be of great interest to the U.S. private sector. The oil industry is a cardinal focus of such concern. Until 1988, Burma carefully avoided allowing foreign oil firms to participate in onshore exploration. They were limited to offshore test drilling, which did not prove successful, except for a major find of natural gas in the Gulf of Martaban. That reserve was large enough to exploit, but it would have taken enormous foreign exchange (early estimates were US$1 billion) and local costs and talent, at a time when the international market was soft and there were many regional competitors.

With the Burmese opening of their economy and encouragement of foreign joint ventures in onshore drilling, there has been a renewed spurt of U.S. interest in the Burma market. The halt in U.S. governmental assistance has not discouraged business exploration, nor has the State Department done so. The U.S. interest is shared by entrepreneurs from other nations as well, and it is evident that there was a significant increase in business travel to Burma from late 1988 throughout 1989. Coca Cola, for example, is considering establishing a bottling operation in Burma.

In 1986 US$3.3 million worth of Burmese clothing was exported to the United States (total exports to the United States that year equaled US$13.9 million). By 1988 this figure had risen to US$6.5 million, so that textile quotas were imposed. There are still many obstacles to successful joint ventures in Burma, and U.S. corporations may prove to be less willing than those in other countries to put up initial capital and to await long-term returns in an environment that is still unstable. However, two U.S. oil companies, Amoco and Unocal, received contracts in 1989 for onshore oil exploration.

U.S. interest in Burma's democracy was well received by the populace in 1988. Both because of its location across from the Rangoon city hall and because of its symbolizing of democratic principles, the U.S. embassy was the focal point of many of the antigovernment demonstrations at that time. Before the coup and after, congressional resolutions calling for democracy in Burma were widely publicized, and the Voice of America was listened to with enthusiasm. Because the United States was seen as a prime mover in the termination of foreign assistance by many nations and organizations after the coup, the Burmese military has since shown a coolness to the United States that contrasts with the warmth of the general public. There have been continuous veiled but nevertheless unmistakable criticisms of the United States in the Burmese press, including charges of interference in Burmese internal affairs. General Khin Nyunt has complained that the student dissidents had been reading Henry David Thoreau's *Civil Disobedience*.

U.S. national interests in Burma are thus broadly concerned with poverty, human rights, and political participation. More specifically, they are focused first on narcotics control, then on possible openings for the U.S. business community. To encourage political liberalization, a bill restricting U.S. entry for Burmese products (especially teak and shrimp) was proposed in the U.S. Congress, but it is still in committee. The United States has prevented the commercial shipment of arms to the Burmese government on political and human rights grounds. The Congress has also approved a $250,000 grant for fellowships for Burmese students who have fled Burma.

Tensions exist between the two states, but should a new duly and fairly elected Burmese government be formed, relations would quickly improve. The old impediments to closer relations—U.S. anti-mainland Chinese policies, the cold war, SEATO, Burma's neutrality in the Vietnam War and U.S. involvement in it—are over. But past suspicions remain: missionary links with some rebel leaders, American interest in minority issues, the U.S. base for the opposition Committee for the Restoration of Democracy in Burma, and congressional support for human rights and dissident students. Liberalization could bring into being a new, more fruitful relationship built on popular goodwill.

Yet if the military continues in Burma in some overt and critical role, as now seems likely, and if the elections are viewed as unfair, the United States will be less supportive. Should an anomalous political or human rights situation seem likely to continue indefinitely, then scholarship funds for students to study abroad will continue to be cut off, along with economic assistance and commercial military sales. In addition, lower-level diplomatic contacts may well come under both internal U.S. and international pressure for modification. The United States and other donors would then be faced with the dilemma of the 1970s: Will improving diplomatic relations or increasing foreign assistance encourage change, or the reverse? The Australian position has been to encourage dialogue even before the scheduled elections of May 27, 1990, through continuation of foreign aid and high-level contacts; the U.S., West German, and British position has been the opposite, because such assistance or contacts will not affect the concentration of power in military hands.

Following the elections, however, with the possibility of results that may well be somewhat murky in terms of fairness, the United States and other donors must consider whether the present position of abstinence or renewed assistance would be more conducive to progress. The experience of the 1970s demonstrated, at least at the time, that massive increases in assistance alone will not change policies or induce major reforms. It can be argued that such assistance decreases the likelihood for real reforms by demonstrating to the government that the donors can be relied upon to continue their largess regardless of governmental actions. But an indefinite policy of isolation may not work either. The United States in December 1989 (and secretly as early as July 1989) renewed its high-level contacts with China without any appreciable public evidence of liberalization of Chinese policies. Its inconsistent policies toward Burma and China may become a problem for the United States. Resumption of assistance to Burma without clear reforms there would be a blow to liberalization and better human rights, but refusal to have significant contacts precludes positive U.S. influence. There may not be a satisfactory resolution to this dilemma under conditions in which progress is less than clear-cut. Whatever levels and types of assistance are provided in the future must be negotiated with sensitivity to Burmese perceptions of their own economic and political sovereignty.

VI. Coda: The Future of Burma

The prognosis for Burma is mixed and difficult to assess. The tensions within that complex state are not likely to resolve themselves spontaneously. The process of solution, of course, will never be completed and will inevitably create new difficulties. Yet it is essential to try to discern the future of Burma, and this is an appropriate time to do so, given the trauma Burma has recently experienced and the planned changes in the political and economic structure of the state.

The Western tendency to think in absolutes, universals, and eternal truths may be unsuited to evaluating the Burmese scene. Perhaps one should adopt instead a fundamental Burmese principle, the Buddhist teaching that all is in a state of flux. The official ideology of the BSPP reiterated that theme, noting that even the sacrosanct official party and state dogma might change, as indeed it recently has. The observer of Burmese affairs would be wise to avoid categorical imperatives. The army now appears to be divorced from and hostile to all political parties except the NUP. An abyss seems to separate Burmans from the other ethnic groups. The swing from socialism to capitalism appears complete. But these appearances, among others, may prove ephemeral. The Burmese have demonstrated their capacity to adjust to discordant conditions and to forgive quickly perceived personal or institutional injuries, even though their friendly exterior can mask a shift from placidity to violence with few intermediate stops.

A few generalizations about Burma are likely to remain valid over time. One is that whatever else happens and however much foreign influence is present, the Burmese will deal with these issues in their own manner and at their own pace. They will attempt to retain what they regard as their unique cultural heritage, and with it their comfortable, but if necessary abstemious, lifestyle. Foreign influence will grow. But as this influence inevitably increases for economic reasons and in response to changing communications technology, Burmese cultural atavism will also become apparent. Many Burmese will then reendorse their cultural past or an idealized version of it, perhaps creating a new amalgam suited to their particular needs and setting up barriers to international ethnic or cultural assimilation. In the short term there will likely be more cultural conflicts.

More concretely, the gradual waning of Ne Win's influence will both free the state and create new problems. It will enable policies to be made without the need to conform to Ne Win's whims or to what others think his whims might be. With his departure, the state will also be less cohesive. In the short term, Ne Win cannot be replaced as a symbol. His popularity in some circles will continue, even though he was hated by many and his regime drove the potentially richest nation in Southeast Asia to become the poorest. He has played a unique role in Burma's past.

Burma's leadership will continue to be a critical issue. Five years ago one could predict with a high degree of certainty that the new leadership of Burma would come from the military. Today, that view would have to be amended. The military will be important, indeed vital, but we have seen in the past year the rise in popularity of nonmilitary figures, such as Aung San Suu Kyi. (Of course, her father's military—almost mystical—image made her fame possible.) Likewise, those with military training, such as discharged or retired officers, will also continue to have influence. It is significant that Aung San Suu Kyi's key colleagues are General Tin Oo and Colonel Kyi Maung as well as other retired military figures.

Burma's younger military officers who will inherit positions of power under any future regime will inevitably be better educated than their superiors, and they may have a more academic, less practical understanding of the world. To date, this generation of officers has had little opportunity to study abroad. It is unclear whether, not having fought for independence, they will be more or less nationalistic than the Ne Win generation, but their patriotism should not be in doubt.

Some of the new leaders over the next decade may come from the sons and daughters of the present military leadership. In a sense, we are witnessing the solidification of class through the roles of the children of the previous elites: the children of the present military may assume positions of authority within Burma, while the children of the earlier civilian elites, in exile, are leaders of the opposition abroad.

The military will probably continue to view its role as ensuring national unity and the geographic integrity of the state. The convenience of discussing the military in the singular, however, should not obscure its potential plurality. Without an overbearing father figure at the top, the military may divide on political issues. Officers acting individually or in small groups may unofficially back various political parties to ensure the continuing influence of the military should it appear that the government party could not succeed in a fair election. Of course, many probably do not want to see such an election held, or if held, fairly conducted. Whatever happens, military influence is unlikely to disappear. If Burma is to resolve its military crisis, it will have to deal with the issue of possible retribution for the events of 1988. Any new civilian government not aligned with the military will somehow have to placate the Burmese military about potential retaliation. What will happen to Ne Win will have to be meticulously negotiated.

Whatever political scenarios evolve, factionalism will almost certainly dominate civilian and military life. The perennial smallness of Burma's ruling elites, the personalization of power, the lack of effective autonomous institutions, and the need for patrons and protection in a country that lacks both meritocratic systems and enforced civil rights all point to a continuation of this trend.

Under highly volatile conditions where rent-seeking activities may provide greater opportunities than productive enterprises, those with power who engage in such pursuits and who are perceived to be unfairly wealthy will be the objects of envy. This could further increase political strife, social unrest, and the desire of factions for power.

The events of 1988 make it exceedingly difficult for any authoritarian government, except under conditions of martial law (as presently exist), to maintain extended dictatorial rule. It is quite possible that in the election, which is likely to be held on schedule on May 27, 1990, no single party or group of parties will win a stable majority. This will increase the maneuvering for political alliances and decrease the likelihood of political stability. Thus, any new elected government in Burma will probably be weak. Moreover, even in a civilian government, or in a period of constitutional preparation prior to the formation of such a government, the military will likely continue to play a large role. A stable, politically balanced democracy is not necessarily the only alternative to the present military dictatorship. It is quite possible that the NUP with its rural network and ample funding will do well in an election, especially in rural constituencies, but its credibility may be in question.

Any new government, either one organized by the NUP on behalf of the present government or one in which the military retains ultimate authority, will probably have to make some nonmilitary gestures toward the insurgents. This is an area that the military command will watch with great care, and in which it is likely to be involved. Concessions will have to be made toward some type of federal or power-sharing system, although the balance will almost certainly remain with the center and with the Burman majority.

94

Should any minority coalition demand too much autonomy, then more traditional Burman elements such as the *sangha*, in addition to the military, are likely to protest. It is also likely that no group will be satisfied with any compromise, at least in the early stages. How to ameliorate such dissatisfactions and adjudicate disputes will be a primary issue. At best the process of resolution will be slow and stormy.

The most probable five-year scenario would place the military in continuing influence and thus substantial power after the elections of May 1990, since the elections are likely to be for a type of constitutional convention, with the *tatmadaw* continuing to run the state apparatus or retaining ultimate authority until a constitution is formulated and a referendum, and then perhaps another election, held. From that position, they could directly influence the constitutional process. They are liable to be in command until about 1992, after which retired military officers are likely to play critical roles in a civilian regime.

Meanwhile, the current government's opening to the private sector is real and necessary. The need for such an opening has been a recurrent theme since independence. Usually the openings have come too slowly and have been less than effective. Now the current economic conditions of the government as well as its political need to enhance state legitimacy, give a new dimension to this recurring problem; thus the effort to encourage the private sector will be more thorough, and probably more effective. Yet the government does not understand the nature of international business, nor the conditions under which long-term investment will be made. Thus it considers its new foreign investment law to be very liberal, "the best investment law in the world," according to the minister of trade, whereas the law actually leaves many issues vague or unanswered. To develop a better understanding will require more exposure to the international scene, which will undercut Burma's traditional economic autonomy and require greater concessions to the external business community. In a reasonably open political system, with a free press, such activities would probably be denounced by the left as destructive of state independence. This argument might even carry weight if the concessions did not produce the desired result. In South Korea, the startling and continuing economic gains for the population as a whole have limited the effectiveness of such criticism. Burma's new openness to the outside will also be criticized internally if income disparities grow and become obvious, a likely product of economic growth.

Internally, it is likely that the minority groups, the Chinese, and those from the Indian subcontinent will gain a greater share of the economic pie than the Burmese, for all the reasons previously discussed. More important, they will be perceived as gaining an even greater share than they actually do, especially if the economy expands rapidly. This is an area where deftly designed incentives—economic, training, tax, and political—might alleviate a problem before it arises. If early attention is not given to this issue, there may well be a return to communal problems and severe internal economic trauma. The Indian and Sino-Burmese communities may well be the new middle class in Burma—but how Burma will handle this political problem remains to be seen.

The role of foreign institutions, both private businesses and aid agencies, will be critical in Burma's future economy. If reasonably fair elections are held, foreign assistance will come pouring back into Burma. If strict standards for use of that aid are not enforced, and if policy discussions are not held and the Burmese are unwilling to have such a dialogue, then Burma will likely return to its previous haphazard economic planning. Donors, for their own internal bureaucratic reasons, tend to spend at predetermined budget levels based on their own needs rather than on recipient absorptive capacities or policy reforms. It would be unfortunate if this tendency were to outweigh the need for careful economic planning and policy reforms.

As the world's largest donor to Burma and Burma's previous main support, Japan has a special role in Burma's future. If Japanese spending levels are determined on the basis of non-Burmese needs, this will allow the Burmese government to avoid making the harsh economic decisions that have to be made, resulting in piecemeal and less-than-effective reforms. This is essentially what happened in the 1970s. Both the Burmese and their foreign donors should insist on phased, consistent economic reform measures so that Burma will prosper.

As a safety valve against political and economic pressures, Burma has allowed more citizens to emigrate since the mid-1970s. This trickle has become a strong stream. Burma is losing many of its most talented and educated people, who see little economic opportunity and, at least until 1989, not much political hope in their native land. When other countries became serious about economic growth, they tried to attract back those who had left. South Korea was quite successful. Burma will have to do something similar, but under a liberalized political and economic structure that encourages trained and dedicated people. Now, Burma has lost an entire talented generation.

As urbanization increases, Burma's political boiling point may well drop. The administrative capacity of the state will have to grow to supply the needs of the burgeoning urban population who, separated from their rural support, must rely on the government to supply their daily living requirements. The government will have to develop a meritocratic civil service if it is to deal with these issues, one that is not bound by political loyalties to leaders, as has been the case throughout contemporary Burma. This process requires time, but there is little left in which to make government effective in Burma.

With growing urbanization will probably come two developments, both of which will test the acumen of any new regime. These are the need for increased and meaningful urban employment at levels commensurate with education, and the growth of institutions free of government control. Currently, educated Burmese find few opportunities for positions using their considerable skills. In addition, Burmese have been reluctant to form civic or other groups in the past unless they were associated with religious functions or mandated by government. Increased urbanization and the development of a more complex economy will encourage the expansion of these organizations, which will likely be professionally oriented, and which will offer the beginning of nongovernmental and plural centers of influence. Although a slow process, the growth of these groups, which are flourishing in other countries in the region, will reinforce tendencies toward political pluralism, although they cannot be seen as a panacea for Burma's political needs.

This author has accepted the government's commitment to elections as real. But prevention of three of the four leading candidates from participating in the elections poses serious questions about the efficacy of the process and the value of the results. The destruction of the leadership of the National League for Democracy has undercut the SLORC's credibility and commitment, while its wholesale arrests and intelligence network have created widespread fear. If changes in SLORC attitudes do not soon become apparent, then there will be an even more significant malaise in the postelection period.

Although it is hazardous to predict the rise of strong individual leaders, it is likely that, as in the past, such a leader will arise in the next few years. This individual could operate within a multiparty or democratic context, but the Burmese political system may well force him or her to strive to govern beyond factions and entourages. Such a person, operating with competence and within the appropriate political milieu, might provide the stimulus for Burmese progress, for progress is what all concerned observers of Burma hope for at this time. Strong leadership in Burma need not mean autocratic rule, although it has done so in the past; rather, it might result from a personal, progressive vision and an aura of cultural relevance within a pluralistic system. The impact of individual influence on Burmese policies should not be underestimated.

Burma is also likely to be the center of regional power rivalries as its economy opens. It will need to consider how best to preserve its freedom amongst these important groups; how to avoid too early and too complete commitments; and—with an eye toward its internal political process—how to prevent the public perception that the government has sold out to a neighbor.

The essential issue is not how foreigners, however well-wishing, may regard Burma, nor how theoretically sound their analyses. Rather, it is how well these foreign perspectives conform to Burmese conceptions of their own society. Whatever road Burma chooses, and whatever the results, action will be taken *bama-lo*, in the Burmese manner.

Suggested Reading

Note: This list only includes social-science works that are devoted to Burma in the military period since 1962. For a more complete bibliography, see The Wilson Center, The Smithsonian Institution, Asia Program, *Burma: A Study Guide* (Washington, DC: 1987). For a more selective bibliography for the pre-1982 period, see "Suggested Reading" in David I. Steinberg, *Burma: A Socialist Nation of Southeast Asia* (Boulder: Westview Press, 1982).

Lehman, F. K., ed., *Burma Under the Military: A Kaleidoscope of Views* (Singapore: Maruzen Asia [for the Institute of Southeast Asian Studies], 1981).

Lintner, Bertil, *Outrage* (Hong Kong: Review Publishing Co., 1989).

Lintner, Bertil, *The Rise and Fall of the Communist Party of Burma (CPB)* (Ithaca: Cornell University, Southeast Asia Program [in press]).

Maung Maung Gyi, *Burmese Political Values: The Socio-Political Roots of Authoritarianism* (New York: Praeger Publishers, 1983).

Silverstein, Josef, *Burma: Military Rule and the Politics of Stagnation* (Ithaca: Cornell University Press, 1977).

Silverstein, Josef, ed., *Independent Burma at Forty Years: Six Assessments* (Ithaca: Cornell University, Southeast Asia Program, 1989).

Steinberg, David I., *Burma's Road Toward Development: Growth and Ideology Under Military Rule* (Boulder: Westview Press, 1981).

Steinberg, David I., *Burma: A Socialist Nation of Southeast Asia* (Boulder: Westview Press, 1982).

Taylor, Robert H., *The State in Burma* (Honolulu: University of Hawaii Press, 1987).

About the Author

David I. Steinberg is President Emeritus of the Mansfield Center for Pacific Affairs. A former member of the Agency for International Development's Senior Foreign Service, he was educated at Lingan University (Canton, China), Dartmouth College, Harvard University, and the School of Oriental and African Studies, University of London. Mr. Steinberg is the author of many articles, monographs, and books on Burma, Korea, and development, including *Burma's Road Toward Development: Growth and Ideology Under Military Rule* (Westview Press, 1981), *Burma: A Socialist Nation of Southeast Asia* (Westview Press, 1982), and *The Republic of Korea: Economic Transformation and Social Change* (Westview Press, 1989). He has spent more than 15 years in Asia, including 4 in Burma.